Excellence in First-Year Writing

2012/2013

The English Department Writing Program
and
The Gayle Morris Sweetland Center for Writing

Edited by
Alan Hogg and Dana Nichols

Published in 2013 by MPublishing
University of Michigan Library

MPublishing
4186 Shapiro
919 South University
Ann Arbor, MI 48109
lib.pod@umich.edu

ISBN 978-1-60785-295-7

Table of Contents

Excellence in First-Year Writing

Excellence in First-Year Writing 2012/2013

EDWP Writing Prize Committee:

Tim Green, Co-Chair
Stephanie Moody, Co-Chair
Christie Allen
Daphna Atias
Camille Beckman
Kathryne Bevilacqua
Jesse Carr
Jeremiah Chamberlin
Steve Engel
Gail Gibson
Julia Hansen
Josh Kupetz
James Kusher
Bruce Lack
Brian Matzke
Ruth McAdams
Melody Pugh
Logan Scherer
Meg Sweeney
Ann Marie Thornburg
Christie Toth
Jessica Young

Sweetland Writing Prize Chairs:

Alan Hogg
Dana Nichols

Administrative Support:

Laura Schulyer
Hanna Linna

Winners list

Feinberg Family Prize for Excellence in First Year Writing

Audrey Coble: "Dying to Live" *nominated by Joe Horton, English 124*

Willie Filkowski: "Instagarbage" *nominated by Ruth McAdams, English 125*

Sam Naples: "Behind Closed Doors: Why Many Restaurants are Reluctant to Share Basic Information About Their Food to Us – And What We Can Do to Stop It" *nominated by Andrew Bozio, English 125*

Matt Kelley Award for Excellence in First-Year Writing

Yardain Amron: "When the Silence Settles" *nominated by Tim Hedges, LHSP 125*

Amelia Brown: "Ink" *nominated by Tim Hedges, LHSP 125*

Sweetland Prize for Outstanding Writing Portfolio

Trishanya Raju: "Confessions of a Sci-Fi Junkie," "Conforming to Anticonformity," *nominated by Paul Barron, Writing 100*

Grace Yan Sun: "Research Summary 4," "Considerations," *nominated by Simone Sessolo, Writing 100*

Nominees list

Feinberg Family Prize nominees

Student Name	Instructor Name
Jessica Aboukasm	Christine Modey
Brady Akman	Amielle Major
Lauren Allport	Claire Skinner
Melanie Askari	Jessica Young
Amanda Bassett	Amrita Dhar
Ryan Bell	Andrew Bozio
Alec Brabandt	Claire Skinner
Rebecca Brewster	Aubrey Schiavone
Alex Brusher	Jaimien Delp
Jake Cahan	Jessica Young
Julia Campbell	Yamil Avivi
Amy Cook	Tricia Khleif
Emma DeJonge	Joe Horton
Charles Dotson	Francine Harris
Ian Forman	Ann Marie Thornburg
Jennifer Gabo	Francine Harris
Max Goldberg	Garrett Felber
Cassidy Goldblatt	Ann Marie Thornburg
Andrew Gordner	Francine Harris
Alex Grombala	Jessica Young
Jordan Joersz	Jessica Young
Samantha Jones	Trevor Kilgore
Matt Kaufman	Russell Brakefield
Jesse Kelley	Joe Horton
Kara Kitze	Sarah Allison

Megan Klatt	Gail Gibson
Richard Klein	Anna Sheaffer
Samantha Lentz	Francine Harris
Jessica Leshman	Gail Gibson
Molly Liebeskind	David Ward
Will Lobb	Sarah Allison
Sam Mancina	Jennifer Tomscha
Jordan Miller	Jessica Young
Andrea Montoya	Ruth McAdams
Iris Mustich	Aubrey Schiavone
Suhail Noor	Jessica Young
Mark Ossolinski	Joe Horton
Carly Paull-Baird	David Ward
Andrew Padula	Patrick Barry
Hallie Parker	Daphna Atias
Tanner Porter	Tricia Khleif
Samrudh Rajachudamani	Francine Harris
Carrie Ramseyer	Trevor Kilgore
Johnny Richards	Kathryne Bevilacqua
Morgan Sandelski	Garrett Felber
Penny Savryn	Amrita Dhar
Shelby Senna	Jennifer Tomscha
Emily Shrosbree	Jessica Young
Kushal Singh	James Kusher
Al Smith	Joe Horton
Matthew Spector	Patrick Barry
Dylan Spiro	Francine Harris
Mike Stein	Jessica Young
Michael Stinavage	Christie Allen
Ali Thomason	Jessica Young

Melanie Toney	Adam Sneed
Samuel Torchio	Erin Baribeau
Eric Totaro	Ruth McAdams
Kit Trowbridge	Jenny Kohn
Alicia Venchuk	Cordelia Zukerman
Danielle Wallick	Jessica Young
Julia Walsh	Ruth Anna Spooner
Abigail Wang	Mélissa Gélinas
David Weinfeld	Amielle Major
Jacob Wolf	Jaimien Delp

Matt Kelley Prize nominees

Student name	**Instructor name**
Jessica Aboukasm	Christine Modey
Yardain Amron	Tim Hedges
Holly Armstrong	Barbara Sloat
Amelia Brown	Tim Hedges
Rachel Bruck	Mark Banaszak Holl
Elyse Brusher	Clara Bosak-Schroeder
Samuel Cusimano	Clara Bosak-Schroeder
Melissa Daily	Christine Modey
Michael Ding	Maria Hadjipolycarpou
Hannah Feldshuh	Harriet Fertik
Evan Gennrich	Helen Dixon
Madeline Herman	Mark Banaszak Holl
Ryan Kuesel	Spencer Hawkins
Nikila Lakshmanan	Carl Cohen
Tiffany Liu	Mark Banaszak Holl
Gunnar Moll	Maria Hadjipolycarpou

Ashwini Natarajan	Barbara Sloat
Aubrey O'Neil	Paul Barron
Connor Rademaker	Carl Cohen
Erin Rogers	Rostom Mesli
Allison Schneider	Paul Barron
Benjamin Toll	Carl Cohen
Claire Wiggins	Harriet Fertik
Lauren Wood	Spencer Hawkins

Portfolio prize nominees

Student Name	Instructor Name
Haya Alfarhan	Scott Beal
Leonard Ang	Jennifer Metsker
Sierra Ayres	Paul Barron
Karen Marie Bates	Simone Sessolo
Molly Breen-Bondie	Julie Babcock
Audriana Buchanan	Gina Brandolino
Zachary Cohn	Gina Brandolino
Savannah Dakota	Lila Naydan
Megan Dotson	Barron, Paul
Kayla Hanses	Tim Hedges
Danica Harris	Lila Naydan
Ethan Koshar	Scott Beal
Sophia Lee	Elizabeth Gramm
Alan McKelton	Kelly Allen
Jillian Mills	Sarah Allison
Harshana Perera	Jennifer Metsker
Sang Phung	Julie Babcock
Alex Quinlan	Lila Naydan

Trishanya Raju	Barron, Paul
Sam Sirotkin	Elizabeth Gramm
Grace Sun	Simone Sessolo
Bruce Szudera Wienand	Scott Beal

Introduction

For writers, one of the most challenging and rewarding activities is to engage with other writers' work. We learn a tremendous amount from exploring how writers formulate questions, respond to other thinkers, appeal to their readers, utilize evidence, create beautiful phrases and images, and participate in meaningful conversations. At the University of Michigan, our introductory composition courses foster such engagement through peer review workshops, which help students to identify themselves and each other as writers. In an effort to celebrate this kind of work, the English Department Writing Program and the Sweetland Center for Writing established a first-year writing prize in 2010. With generous support from the Sweetland Center for Writing and from Andrew Feinberg and Stacia Smith, both of whom earned English degrees from the University of Michigan, we honor students who have produced writing of exceptional quality, and we share their work so that other writers may learn from, and feel inspired by, their examples.

Like the writing process, which involves strengthening our writing through conversation with other writers, selecting and publishing these prize-winning essays entailed extensive conversation among a range of writers. Articulating why a particular selection merited a prize was both challenging and illuminating, and it helped to sharpen the writerly perceptions of all who participated. The electronic portfolios produced in Sweetland's Writing 100 were read and discussed by Christine Modey, Simone Sessolo, Naomi Silver,

Lila Naydan, Ray McDaniel, and Dana Nichols. Entries for the Matt Kelley Prize for Excellence in First-Year Writing were read and discussed by Louis Cicciarelli, Dave Karcynski, Jamie Jones, Carol Tell, Scott Beal, Tim Hedges, and Dana Nichols. Entries for the English Department Writing Program's Feinberg Family Writing Prize were read and discussed by Christie Allen, Jesse Carr, Daphna Atias, James Kusher, Camille Beckman, Christie Toth, Steve Engel, Kathryne Bevilacqua, Gail Gibson, Jessica Young, Julia Hansen, Bruce Lack, Brian Matzke, Ann Marie Thornburg, Ruth McAdams, Logan Scherer, Melody Pugh, Josh Kupetz, Jeremy Chamberlin, and Meg Sweeney, with Tim Green and Stephanie Moody serving as chairs of the committee. We are deeply grateful to all of these writers for sharing their time and expertise.

Equally deserving of thanks are the many students who submitted essays for the first-year writing prize and the instructors who encouraged and supported them. This year's particularly difficult selection process reminded us of the wonderful work that happens every day in hundreds of university writing classes. As writing teachers, we feel grateful for our many opportunities to learn from the challenging questions, intellectual energy, creativity, and dedication that our students and their teachers bring to our classrooms.

Anne Ruggles Gere, Director, Sweetland Center for Writing
Meg Sweeney, Director, English Department Writing Program

Feinberg Family Prize for Excellence in First-Year Writing

It is with great pleasure that we present this year's winning essays of the Feinberg Family Prize for Excellence in First Year Writing. The following essays, written by students taking English 124 or 125 in 2012, represent outstanding examples of complex, analytic arguments that matter in academic contexts. These essays were selected from a group of seventy impressive submissions and passed a rigorous, multi-round judging process. Our selection committee, composed of twenty-two writing instructors, carefully read and evaluated each essay; given the caliber of the submission pool, the decision process was incredibly difficult. Nevertheless, these essays stood out as superior examples of academic writing by first-year students.

The first-year writing course is a foundational experience for UM students. It is intended to introduce students to academic skills that will help them succeed as they navigate the varied disciplines, academic genres, and ways of knowing represented in higher education. Although instructors of first-year writing can design their courses in a number of ways, all courses ask students to write a variety of texts, produce academic arguments based in analysis and supported by close reading and research, and demonstrate awareness of rhetorical situations and conventions. Most importantly, all first-year writing courses foster academic inquiry and promote writing as a means of learning about and engaging with the world.

The essays featured here reflect a variety of genres and rhetorical contexts, from personal narrative to investigative report to socio-historical analysis. What they share, however, is a commitment to exploring a topic of interest through rigorous inquiry, reflection, and research. Through careful analysis, each author sets on a path toward discovering an answer to a thoughtful and complex question: how to make sense of an atypical – and life-changing – work experience, how to engage in ethical and sustainable eating practices, and what to make of technological advancements that synthetically manufacture the past. We invite you join these students on their journeys and to grapple with these same questions.

Stephanie Moody and Tim Green
Co-Chairs of Feinberg Family First-Year Writing Prize Committee
Graduate Student Mentors, English Department Writing Program

Dying to Live

From English 124: Audrey Coble (nominated by Joe Horton)

Audrey's essay comes from the personal narrative portion of our class, and was the second the four essays written in the term. Authors were encouraged to use their own "raw material of life" (what Vivian Gornick calls the situation) in service of creating a larger argument or supporting a larger worldview (Gornick's story). In my teaching career, I have not read a student essay better than Audrey's in its use of both situation and story. Here, Audrey not only uses her experiences working in a morgue to ask serious and far-reaching questions about life and death, but she shows her awareness of the process of writing. Her eagerness to have something to write leads to a far more profound realization of what it means to think you don't have anything to write. Life and death are heady topics indeed, but Audrey's writing is both detailed and welcoming; she leads us through this unfamiliar and perhaps frightening environment with skill and grace. Like the best personal narratives (and indeed the best writing, period), we feel simultaneously supported and challenged by Audrey, and we as readers learn about the world and question our place in it almost effortlessly. She is a hugely gifted writer who, as evidenced by this essay, has come to understand that good subject matter is a blessing and a curse.

Joe Horton

Dying to Live

The pathologist nods and I take a steadying breath, trying not to choke on the smell, and look at the man on the table. I grasp one of his wrists with my left hand and cross my right hand over my left, stretching to clutch his hip with it. I hoist him up on his side, my shoes sliding inside of their sterile shoe covers on the linoleum floor. The arms of the man on the table are long, so his fingers just touch the plastic apron that covers my stomach. Every time he starts to slide onto his back again, I have to stutter, let go for a minute, and grip tighter.

He's dead.

Both of my grandfathers died long before I was born, when my parents were teenagers. When I was in second grade, my paternal grandmother—a smart, sharp, and funny woman who suffered from multiple sclerosis for some forty years—passed away. My mother delivered the news with tears in her eyes after picking us up from school one day, and I received the news with only partial understanding. I knew what death meant, technically: death meant a silent heart, death meant a place in the sky and a hole in the ground, death meant a long, cold absence and pounds of dark wet dirt. Death meant the first time I'd ever seen my dad cry. Past these tiny details, I failed to grasp the big picture. My mother didn't want us to go to the funeral because she wanted us to remember our grandmother how she had been when we last visited her: alive.

Years later, when I was a senior in high school, the time came to choose where I'd do my Senior May Program, a program at my high school comprised of a mandatory, month-long internship at any business or organization I chose. When it came time to write my proposals, I immediately remembered the presentations several students in the classes before me had given on their experiences at the morgue, which ranged from exciting to life-changing: after her month at the morgue, one of the students actually changed her whole major and course of study in order to become a coroner. When I told my mother I wanted to do my senior year internship at the coroner's office, she gave me a startled look and nearly screamed at me before frantically offering alternatives. In Chinese culture, it's extremely unlucky to speak about death in any circumstance; and having lived through the Chinese Cultural Revolution, my mother had likely seen more than her share of death already. Once or twice, when I was young, I asked her if she had friends when she was a child, like I did, because she never seemed to mention them. My mother would look at me and shake her head, then start a story about her neighbor, before stopping and choking up. Not knowing any better, I would reach out to grab her arm and naively ask, "Mommy? What happened?" Her answer was always, "I don't want to talk about it. Those days are over. He was a good man, and he always helped us." Afterwards, the air would be thick and swollen with welling memories, too much emotion in the small space between us.

These moments always haunted me until I read books on the Cultural Revolution for class in middle school that described my mother's experiences. Sons and daughters publically humiliated and denounced, their mothers and fathers seized, simply vanished, made to turn against their families and friends, and then tortured and executed anyway. My mother never told me explicitly, but I knew from her stories and the memories that never fully made their way into words that she had seen friends, family, classmates, and neighbors disappear. She had seen family members returned, completely silenced as a result of the beatings. My mother knew death. Death had touched her life, and she wanted to protect me from all of the hurt and pain she had seen.

Looking back, I see her intent; but as we argued, I did not have the words to thank her, nor to tell her that seeking out the dead was something I needed to do to better understand myself, my world, and perhaps even her world. So, I would sigh as she would ask variations on the same frenzied questions over and over: "Why don't you work in my friend's lab instead? She works with bacteria." She didn't realize I'd already decided on the coroner's office without a doubt. "Why would you want to work with dead people every day?" I would shrug. I didn't actually know, but something drew me to the job; not only because a stint at the morgue had changed the lives of those who worked there before me, but also because I felt some sense that the dead might have some sort of answers or that the corpses might have something to teach me, about writing or about life.

I felt my duty as a writer was to live as uniquely as possible, to collect swaths of raw experience to distilled into meaning, experience, language, and beauty for myself and for my future readers. When I announced to my friends and teachers that I planned to work at the morgue, their offhand remarks that "I must be braver, or a different sort of person" only served to encourage me. When they asked me how I would stand the sight of all that blood, I quickly realized I would do it because I had to. I had to know, I had to learn, I had to understand. And in my writing, consequentially, my readers would know that I had seen death for myself, and they, too, could know, and they could learn, and they could understand. Inside, behind my passion and apparent courage, part of me squirmed, uncomfortable with the fact that I would be so selfish as to want to use the deaths of others. I had to wonder if I was only using my readers as an excuse to allow myself unrestrained participation in morally blurry experiences. Honestly, I could not extricate my own want from my desire to teach readers, and even after months of considering and reconsidering, I still have not reached a conclusion. I had seen death peripherally, but in order to truly select the correct details and to translate experience to writing, I would have to understand death first. However I could never explain these vague, ill-developed thoughts to my mom, so I would simply shrug. "I don't know." She would shake her head in response, trying to invoke my father's disapproval as well. Some days, her question was simply, "But why?"

The man on the table's hands are freezing—actually freezing, as he came out of a freezer just moments ago—and my hands are going numb through the latex of the double-layered surgical gloves I'm wearing. (Think of holding a frozen steak.) The pathologist finally nods and I let go, the body clanging rigidly back into place on the metal autopsy table. At this point, I am still careful to be absolutely sure that I'm wiping what I call "corpse juice"—what's really water leaking from the body's cells—onto my smock instead of my skin, leaving two cold wet streaks on the blue plastic. I step back, having done my part, and look around: the bright light reflects off of the metal autopsy table and glints into my eyes. The walls are blue, and scales for weighing organs hang above each table. Giant silver industrial sinks equipped with powerful spray hoses line the walls, and a doublewide metal door marks the entrance to the large walk-in freezer where shelves of bodies are kept.

Everyone inside this room is suited in exactly the same way as I am. Before I could even enter the morgue, I was handed a pair of severe black scrubs with the coroner's office's seal ironed neatly on the front right side, and told to bring a pair of liquid-proof "dirty shoes" that I wouldn't mind getting bloody. Then, I was ushered into the morgue to put on the rest of the gear: shoe covers, latex gloves, a long-sleeved knee-length plastic smock that tied at the back and stretched over my thumbs, and a second pair of longer surgical gloves over top of the latex gloves and the cuffs of the smock. Lastly, I was given a surgical mask, safety glasses, and a hair cover. Once fully suited in protective gear, I was briefly lectured about the risks of catching Hepatitis A and B, AIDS, and other blood-and-fluid borne illnesses.

Finally, I was ready.

A forensic technician leads me into the morgue, where six other technicians and pathologists stand around a body, with only their eyes visible behind their clear plastic safety glasses. The pathologist adjusts and readjusts the mask covering his nose and mouth, and I wonder: perhaps these pathologists, weathered doctors who had practiced medicine in South Africa in a time before masks or gloves were even recommended, let alone required, are not afraid of disease. They constantly complain about the inconveniences the masks and gloves cause, and they proclaim repeatedly that they are not afraid of contamination from blood or fecal matter or stomach contents. So why, then, insist on wearing the extra-thick surgical smock? Why still use long, double layered surgical gloves? Finally, I realize.

They are afraid of death.

And I am, too. For all of my bravado, my justifications and reasoning, the layer of sticky sweat starting to form between my skin and the plastic of the smock still feels like safety. Two or three pairs of rubber gloves on each hand prevent my fingers from bending and protect my blood from potential infection, but also seal my living flesh off from any contact with the dead, decomposing flesh before me. A mask rests over my mouth and nose so no bodily fluids can spatter into my mouth and make me sick, but also so that I don't breathe any particles that may have come from the cadaver itself, or any essence of death that might have floated up and out of the body while we were turned the other way. We suit up to prevent bacteria, of course, but we also suit up to prevent spiritual infection, to prevent emotional infection, to make a physical declaration of our separation from the dead who share our space and our thoughts. I want to see death before me, but I do not want to catch it. I want to be near it, to be nearly in touch with it, but still be safely sealed off and protected from any contact. I feel weak.

The first time I attended an autopsy, I watched the process from a few feet back, simultaneously trying not to breathe and to acclimate myself to the distinctly human smell of feces, urine and a sweet, sugary, candy-and-rot smell that you would never expect days-old blood to have. The smell is partially blocked by the face mask covering my nose and mouth, and I am incredibly thankful for the mint smell of my brushed-teeth breath. This smell of dead bodies is one part of the experience Hollywood never captures: the scent of a corpse is incredibly distinctive, extremely strong, and impossible to ignore. Lessons from the Hollywood and the media: people die often.

People die dramatically. People die. In action movies, in horror movies, on the news broadcast every morning and every evening, in crime thriller television shows, in video games, even in books. And so, I wonder: *why is death such a thrillingly taboo topic? Why is the corpse the representation of the human body we cannot seem to grow comfortable with or forget?*

After my first autopsy, I peeled off layers of sweaty latex and cotton, changed back into my office clothes and sat down at my desk. While I had been in autopsy, someone had laid out a form with a pen crossed neatly on top—a statement I had to sign that prohibited me from speaking, writing, or communicating in any other way any personal identifying details of a decedent's case, even in the private journal I was to keep for credit as a part of my school's program. My hand trembled slightly as I turned the paper in, and as I blinked, the face of corpse whose autopsy I just observed burned behind my eyelids, seared into my mind. Before I had arrived at the morgue, I had counted on being able to *use* my experiences in my writing, had wanted to see the bodies for my characters and for my readers, and to employ a catalogue of details I would pick from the strangest and the most ordinary deaths to bring a decomposing body to the page in a way that would shatter my characters and challenge my readers to call my writing fiction. I had, at the very least, wanted to be able to write stories simply to process everything I was seeing at the morgue. Instead, I found myself struggling to concentrate on the *why* while also fighting to ignore the nauseating smell of dead bodies caught in my nose, attempting to memorize the exact noise made when the renal capsule is peeled back from the kidney itself, and choking down my lunch of yogurt with a mix-in strawberry blend the color and consistency of human entrails. I sat at the desk and blinked a few lethargic times, allowing the image of the man's face to possess my vision and my thoughts. Every time my eyes slipped shut, my mind clutched desperately tighter to the memories of the autopsy: I felt somehow that I was duty-bound to save these bits of sensation until I could find a way to write them down, for the sake of the man whose autopsy I had just watched. Without being able to tell his story—or, at least, the story I had created for him; soaring, touching, and deeply meaningful—storing these snapshots of him and his rigid body until they could be recorded seemed the best and only way I could thank him for letting me be there, for letting me see him vulnerable and exposed, for letting me learn from him and take his secrets back to the living. If I could not give him a *why*, I could at least preserve the *how*. My journal entry for the day read: Attended first autopsy for 2.5 hours; learned how to dress protectively to prevent disease; tried to get used to the smell.

The next day, in the same linoleum-floored room, a woman—one of the only people whose self I knew before I saw her body cut open and emptied, slopped into a plastic biohazardous waste bag. She was an alcoholic, and one day on her walk home from the bar, she tripped up a hill and fell, hitting her head hard enough to cause bleeding, and landing with her neck pressed to a foot-tall timber that marked the border of a garden on the edge of a deserted lot. Because she was drunk and unconscious, she was not able to move, and died of asphyxiation. She came to the morgue with her head bent to one side, rigid and awkward, and the imprint of the wood red and raw on her neck. I watch the pathologist try to snap her neck back into position, watch the forensic technician line up a ruler and photograph the wound, and I wonder why she became an alcoholic. I wonder if she was the type of talented person who was too torturously smart to live in her own mind, and whether alcohol helped slow or dull or soften or stop his thoughts for her when she or sleep could not. I think about her husband and perhaps a daughter who might have been crying but might not have been crying because she was about to destroy their family. I stare at the layer of fat between skin and muscle, hardened differently than usual, and the extra tissue connecting her intestines to the walls of her abdomen; all because of the excess of alcohol she drank. I wonder if she, given the chance, would have chosen to come back to life. Inside of myself and all of the books I had read and all of the movies I had watched, I look for her. I see the brain through the opened-up skull and I wonder what made this woman different from every book and every movie, what made her the same. I wonder if she can see herself. I wonder if she was happy. I wonder if she is happy. Behind my safety glasses I close my eyes and try to hear and taste on my tongue the one secret *no one* knew that she was hoarding for her deathbed confession. I try to make myself permeable and allow a wisp of her memory to enter me and show me how she thought she would die. The pathologist slices open her neck and starts to examine it, and I wonder: why do accidental things happen to brilliant people? *Why must our lives end in such abject horror?*

After a full-body external examination and collection of blood, vitreous, and urine, the body is cut open. Organs are removed, dissected, examined for any irregularities or signs of trauma or disease. As I watch the doctor reach through the slop to fish out the kidneys or the lungs or the pancreas, I wonder how all those people who have never seen the inside of a person can live without this knowing. The scientist in me is observing, taking in the position of the organs, their color and weight and texture and consistency, drawing comparisons to anatomy textbooks and Hollywood special effects and science classes and Google Images, looking for the how. The pathologist quizzes me after removing the organs:

"How do you think this man died? Why?"

These strike me immediately as two very different questions, and at first, I don't have an explanation for either. I don't realize that cocaine causes an enlarged heart or that heroin overdoses often have an excess of fluid in the lungs. But soon, I learn to look for swollen gyri, for subdural hematomas, for blood or excess fluid in the myocardial sac, and attribute them to certain causes of death. Soon after, I'm able read multiple symptoms to identify some of the most common causes of death. The *how* reveals itself.

However, the writer in me, the reader of books where every death is meaningful and symbolic, is still looking for the "real" answers to questions of *why*—of why we die, and in doing so, why we live, why our flitting ideas and philosophies must be housed in pounds of slimy flesh—as though they might be someplace hidden inside everyone. I hold out hope for this even though I know it can't be true, peering over the doctor's shoulder as he slices open the heart to reveal the muscular chambers or carefully plucks the brain out of the skull, delivering it delicately, like a baby, to the cutting board.

The brain is my favorite organ; reaching it requires so much fanfare and the organ itself looks so unassuming. The forensic technicians use a circular bone saw to cut the top of the skull off, peel out the dura, a membrane that covers and protects the brain, and then carefully sever the optic nerves so they can gently tug the brain out and examine it. The outside is beige and the inside stark white, thickly wrinkled over most of its surface and then whorled with intricate lines over parts of the brain stem. The brain has trouble keeping its shape once it's out of the skull, wet and soft, and when cut, it collapses like jello.

Holding a brain in my hands felt like the closest and the farthest I'd ever get to understanding: *Why are we, humans, here?*

In my hands was the absolute center of the human being. In my hands was someone else's life, stories, love, their everything. I was, in essence, holding the entirety of another human being's existence cupped in both palms. I stared at it; bored into it with my eyes, looking for some sort of message, wishing harder than anything that I could read it or that I knew how to interpret it, and that I could just understand.

The pathologist asks for the brain back and I hand it over to him, where he bread-loafs it on the cutting board so he can examine every section for brain damage. When the brain is cut open it is just as beautiful, and the whorls and intricate designs in the brain stem are all the more apparent. The dentate nucleus, a part of the brain stem, is especially striking. Named because the edges are jagged like teeth, the section of the brain resembles a tree or a leaf: a huge vein of white matter diverts into tiny white branches which flower into gray matter. The pathologist cuts little pieces off of the brain stem and some white matter, including the dentate nucleus, plopping them into a little vat of preservative before he dumps the rest of the brain into the waste bucket. He explains that later on, he will make slides from the brain tissue and examine it under the microscope for any signs of disease.

The pathologist's report, however, is the closest I get to seeing any sort of secret in a brain or a heart. Even in the follow-up meetings, we stick strictly to the *how*, and never even discuss the *why*; not even when we get the shocking cases, like babies or murder-suicides. The *why* is simply not our domain. The *why* is not relevant in the processing of the dead, and the *why* could never be answered concretely. There is no room for asking why, because, once asked, it echoes forever.

I found *how* that summer, in many of its variations. I saw dislocated hearts and gunshot wounds and subdural hematomas and overdoses and drownings, I saw hearts and brains and blood, but the corpses never held any real answers. The bodies were devoid of mystery or romanticism—each was processed quickly, dissected and bagged and shipped off to an undertaker, and the whole process lacked the world-stopping weight it did in films and in books. None of it was especially meaningful; none of it was beautiful. Dealing with the dead was a job, just like any other. I had started my internship at the morgue hoping to find some universal answer or secret that all the other authors and philosophers before me had missed, or at least a source of raw, rich material that I could easily write into my short stories. Nevertheless, whenever I opened a blank document or put pen tip to paper, all I had were questions. I found myself creating stories for the bodies I had seen, weaving lives and loves and hope and pain and triumph until I was all too reluctant to finish the story in death, especially deaths as bleak and nauseating as I had seen. Though I did not feel, strictly, that I had failed, I was anxious that I had nothing to teach my readers, nothing different to share, nothing new to describe that I had not already read or seen. Finally disillusioned and ready to stray from my persisting fascination with death, I found myself writing into entirely new territory: I tried my hardest to write about the *living*. I used the bodies I had seen—the *people* I had met—but not in the way I had imagined. I saw these people, I saw their deaths, and then I wrote their lives. The two were intertwined, I found, and though I left with no more answers about death than I had to begin with, I left with so many more questions, I left knowing where to look, and I left with a rekindled desire to ask the question, in all its forms: *Why?*

I realized as I watched a technician sew up the yawning cavity that was a body's hollow torso, maybe the search for meaning and the search for reality actually are separate. Because of the waiver I signed, I have changed the names and identifying details of all of the people and their manners of death. The people in the above narrative verge on the fictional, another few corpses taken from the pile that my family and society adamantly refuses to acknowledge, to speak about, or to forget. My mother and I still have not talked in detail about my time at the morgue, and I know without having to ask not to bring it up with her—the idea of death is still unlucky, still painful for the living. This, I think, is our own version of a nondisclosure waiver.

But my *why* still echoes, a little sharper, a little bit more distinct, and much more real, but still unanswered. The overarching *Why?* I entered the morgue with what had diverted into tens of tiny smaller questions and flowered into speculation. I have come to understand that I do not have an answer to my *Why?* because the questions keep changing and evolving; I saw the questions mirrored in every new organ and every new body, and now, I continue to write and read and *live* in search of more questions, and perhaps even some answers.

Instagarbage

From English 125: Willie Filkowski (nominated by Ruth McAdams)

Willie Filkowski's essay "Instagarbage" is a fascinating meditation on the role of nostalgia in postmodern culture, rich with insights and crackling with a strong argument. He wrote this essay for my section of English 125 that was designed for students in the Living Arts living-learning community at Bursley Hall and organized around the theme "The Arts and the Public." This final essay assignment asked students to make an argument about a problem posed by our artistic heritage in the twenty-first-century world—to explore how the often ideologically problematic art of the past can be understood in the present. Willie's creative interpretation of the prompt turned this question on its head by asking why we use modern technology to create new artistic images that look old.

While Instagram is the specific focus of Willie's discussion, the essay interrogates larger cultural trends and impulses that define our moment. His intelligently selected evidence is supported by an ambitious engagement with writers like Susan Sontag and Frederic Jameson, and indeed, his work makes their ideas seem relevant to technologies that they could not have anticipated. Complementing the strength of his argument, Willie's spirited and provocative writing style results in an essay that is as bracing as it is analytical.

Ruth McAdams

Instagarbage

> "We have a modern notion of embellishment—beauty is not in anything; it is to be found, by another way of seeing—as well as a wider notion of meaning, which photography's many uses illustrate and powerfully reinforce." Susan Sontag, On Photography

In modern culture where the image holds uncontested sway, and where an ever-expanding number of photographers are entering the universe of images, approaches to creation and to aesthetics are up for grabs. Instagram, a massively popular smartphone app and social networking site has staked its claim and asserted its influence on modern picture taking. Without a thought, the Instagram output is catchy and twee. But Instagram wishes to establish a routine way of producing images that is problematic. And it does so in the guise of technological advancement that is truly anything but.

Instagram works in the following way: The user snaps a photo with their smart phone, the Instagram app allows the user to crop the image to a square and apply a filter to the photo, the user applies a caption and an array of "hashtags" and posts it to their feed of images. The idea is that photos come out the other end of the process bursting with layers of visual interestingness and quirky flair. The massive network of users Instagram has then bolsters this quick photo process, which is where the hashtags aid the process. Hashtags are keywords users link to their photos in order that they may be searched. (Instagram has worked hard to encourage specificity in its users' hashtags. "#rustedVW" rather than "#car", "#lobsterrisotto" rather than "#dinner.") Like other social networks, users are able click to like photos and curate a stream of their own.

Instagram's currency is its relationship to nostalgia. Users are so drawn to the application for its ability to place a thick (decades thick) layer of age over recently snapped pictures. The filters can change colors to represent the effects of cross-processed film or a sepia toned print. Users can add borders to make them look like Polaroids or scans from a roll of slide film. With the touch of a finger, users can paint some blur onto the images to forge a shallow depth of field. All of these photo effects are borrowed or exaggerated from specific earlier modes of analogue photography. And this nostalgia seems to dwell in an awkward place: A preponderance of its users are under the age of 29, a demographic whose gargantuan contribution to the site suggests they're nostalgic for an era they haven't even lived.

In examining a similar infatuation with aesthetic modes of a previous era, Paul Grainge attempts to apprehend the '90s' obsession with the black and white image in his *Monochrome Memories: Nostalgia and Style in Retro America*. While tracing the history of the term nostalgia from its origins as a psychological condition to its more contemporary role by way of Fredric Jameson's *Postmodernism: The Cultural Logic of Late Capitalism*, Grainge states,

> In Jameson's theory, nostalgia is not a mood of longing but a "mode" within art, symptomatic of the postmodern "crisis of identity." ... The nostalgia mode does not find utopian meaning in the past, but indiscriminately plunders it for style, refracting the past through fashion and glossy images of "pastness."

If the collective of contemporary picture-takers suffer this crisis of identity (if they are not certain they can contribute to or claim an aesthetic), Instagram provides a way to hedge their insecurities. On the site, photos of mere food are unremarkable. But a photo of mashed potatoes can become coveted if tortured through the right filter and if, since there is no acceptable genuine expression of perceived interestingness, dressed in anemically "retro" off-whites and blaring reds. Plundering for pastness is a one-step process with Instagram.

Uncertain of their aesthetic identities and places as creators, contemporary users of the ever-ready smartphone camera are left with piles of images that they can't be certain are interesting. So they run to Instagram for a solution. Instagram assures users in the frequently asked questions section of its website: "What is Instagram? Instagram is a fun and quirky way to share your life with friends through a series of pictures. Snap a photo with your mobile phone, then choose a filter to transform the image into a memory to keep around forever."

Because the image wasn't good enough when it was first taken. At least, not good enough to be a memory. But Instagram fixes all of this! Instagram gives the world the tools to transform their mere pictures to more immortal mementos and then grants permission to cherish them.

This is infuriating because it encourages a brand of self-consciousness that leaves the world with fewer bold individual choices. It eliminates the risk of being caught out on a limb, having decided that, perhaps a genuine interest in something, expressed by way of a picture, no matter how dim or seemingly untethered in the world of visual tropes, can be stunning as it is. (It's difficult to determine if it's salt in the wound, or if it's a glimmer of hope, but enter the noteworthy #nofilter tag. It's employed when an Instagrammer dares to publish an unfiltered photo. It suggests that there may be unaltered, more direct images that can match the emotional quality of the moment as experienced in the physical world.)

It is no keen act of perception to note the number of photographs taken on film has declined severely or that more and more people are walking through their lives with cellphones possessing increasingly powerful equipment for taking photographs. The technological leaps between the equipment that Instagrammers use to take their photos and the equipment they wish to imitate are huge. And the technology is wonderful. Modern smartphones and their cameras provide opportunities for endless documentation and have not only achieved success in increasing portability and image quality, but they also remove previous barriers like each image costing an appreciable amount of money and time (cost of film, cost of processing, cost of prints, etc.; time spent changing film, time spent developing, time spent editing, etc.)

If photography has come so undoubtedly far with this technology, the question simply must be asked: What is the use, with applications like Instagram, of taking technology's rewards and scampering back in time to validate them? Ian Crouch, in an article titled *Instagram's Instant Nostalgia*, wonderfully identifies many of the results of the Instagram process and simply nails its wonky implementation of the retro aesthetic: it gives "something just a few seconds old the texture of time." It is important to resist the impulse to infuse modern images with this sexy and quirky "pastness" and dig in and find solutions to the challenges posed by technology. It is only through living beyond the time when Instagram's filters were a default look, an honest-to-God product of the era's available tools, that the filters could be seen as styles.

Certainly, like all cultural innovation, there is a process of evolution. Not very much in the cultural landscape can make claim to being parentless. And there is value, aesthetically, in repurposing previous ideas. In considering the social media platform that undergirds Instagram, it's hard to find fault with a system that allows people to easily connect and share with one another. As a tool for design, Instagram is wonderful. It certainly makes it easy to achieve a very specific, and novel aesthetic. And it has its uses. The images are often vivid and compact, and the injection of Instagram magic can lend a sort of ironic credibility to them.

But it becomes dangerous when this becomes the default. When the "Walden" filter is applied, and a white border added, without any regard for its implications, but by virtue of its existence. By the volume of photos added to Instagram daily, and the prevalence of Instagram images in the media, (like a rotating Instagram blog on the *New Yorker's* website) things start to look dicey.

And this criticism is no fear of technology. It's not about an aversion to technology's reduction of time spent working. In fact, it's advocacy for technology. Instagram is not progress. Instagram is cute, but it isn't progress. Instagram is a bit of a plea to turn back the clock. Like few other technical innovations, it doesn't merely make a task quicker and simpler, but it also reduces the quality of the final product. Consider the modern miracle that was the progress from IBM Electromatic Typewriter to Microsoft Word 2007. It's not hard to imagine how the folks behind Instagram, skeptical that the developments of technology have left behind several adorable side effects, would develop a modern word processor: They would, of course, add features that allow the entire thing to crash if a user typed too quickly, and even, every few weeks, allow the program to inexplicably continue to eat space on the page and remain in sync with the typist while nothing was being added to the page – the infinite wonders of a digital dried out ink ribbon!

If Instagram wishes to candy-coat modern life's photographic output and curate it into a series of experiences trapped in a square, with a border and kitschy colors, forever groping toward the past, then Instagram must be answered with lay photographers willing revel in the exceptionalness of reality and photography's innate surreality. There are two ways to respond to the problems posed by Instagram. The first can be found in Sontag:

Photographers need not have an ironic, intelligent attitude toward their stereotyped material. Pious, respectful fascination may do just as well, especially with the most conventional subjects.

The second can be found in time. Instagram asks photographers to sidestep "pious, respectful fascination" with its cheap tricks. There is no reason to allow a smartphone application and social network to act as arbiter and endower of meaning and importance. These tools disregard the intrinsic allure of a photographic reproduction. Instagram offers its users an instantaneous and artificially fabricated replica of something that can only be achieved, and can be achieved most beautifully, by waiting.

References

Crouch, Ian. "Instagram's Instant Nostalgia." *The New Yorker*, 10 Apr. 2012. Web.

Grainge, Paul. *Monochrome Memories: Nostalgia and Style in Retro America.* Westport, CT: Praeger, 2002. Print.

Greenfield, Rebecca. "Rich Kids of Instagram Epitomize Everything Wrong With Instagram." *The Atlantic Wire.* 18 July 2012. Web.

"Instagram." FAQ., Web. 19 Dec. 2012.

Pew Research Center's Internet & American Life Project. *Photos and Videos as Social Currency Online. Pew Internet.* 13 Sept. 2012. Web.

Sontag, Susan. *On Photography.* New York: Farrar, Straus and Giroux, 1977.

Wortham, Jenna. "A Stream of Postcards, Shot by Phone." *New York Times* [New York] 3 June 2011. Web.

Behind Closed Doors: Why Many Restaurants are Reluctant to Share Basic Information About Their Food to Us – And What We Can Do to Stop It

From English 125: Sam Naples (nominated by Andrew Bozio)

Sam's essay reads like a work of investigative journalism. If, in recent years, consumers have become more interested in food sourcing, in whether their groceries are organic or locally grown, then why do we often remain ignorant about where our favorite restaurants find their ingredients? Going in search for answers, Sam blends personal narrative with probing analysis to examine the stakes of what is one of the central paradoxes of contemporary American culture. The obstacles that he encounters are instructive, and they become, in Sam's brilliant analysis, symptomatic of the difficulties we all face in striving to be ethical consumers.

Crucially, Sam's argument balances experiential evidence with research. He locates his own quest within the history of chain restaurants, tracing the growth of an institution so familiar to us in order to show how we, as consumers, might imagine an alternative. This critical genealogy makes Sam's conclusion persuasive, even ineluctable. It's a true testament to the insight and argumentative skill that he brings to bear upon his topic. In short, this essay demonstrates a creativity and an analytical depth that are rare in first-year writing courses, and it reminds us that critical inquiry, sustained analysis, and persuasive writing have important roles to play in shaping our understanding of the world in which we live.

Andrew Bozio

Behind Closed Doors: Why Many Restaurants are Reluctant to Share Basic Information About Their Food to Us—And What We Can Do to Stop it

"You shouldn't eat those! They're so bad for you!" When it comes to the very food we eat, these types of lectures are something we've all been hearing since early childhood, from a wide variety of mouths. Nutritionally, we have been taught by our parents and peers to try to keep things moderate; too many fats can lead to obesity, excessive sodium can prove harmful for our cardiovascular health, etc., so we try to sidestep eating junk-foods and other meals that have overly high levels of these certain components deemed unhealthy. However, nutritional health is only the tip of the iceberg when it comes to the issues to consider when eating. In the twenty-first century, it is no longer enough to understand that chicken has necessarily more essential nutrients than, say, a handful of potato chips. The question of where said chicken came from has become an equally vital piece of knowledge as what the chicken is, when pertaining to our potential food choices. Was it raised on a smaller, organic, free-range farm, or did it grow up in an industrialized stockyard, spending its abridged life in extremely close quarters to thousands of other chickens, being pumped full of antibiotics and growth hormones, under abysmal health conditions, resulting in an exponentially higher risk of carrying foodborne illness to its consumer? Was it shipped to its wholesale buyer from an industrial site 2000 miles away, or from a local farm twenty minutes up the interstate?

The issues here are no secret to the public eye; in fact, they have become so ubiquitous in the last several decades, to the point of being parodied in popular culture as a stereotype of contemporary hipsterism. Still, these relatively new questions—and their subsequent answers—are essential to our ability to behave responsibly and ethically in the modern food environment. And, when shopping for groceries, due to the recent increase in prominence of local farmer's markets and food co-ops, as well as an augmentation of local and organic choices available at supermarkets out of reaction to more ethically conscious customers, it is completely possible to buy healthier, more sustainable, and ultimately more ethical groceries.

But what of the other major source of obtaining food: the restaurant? Eating out is a massive part of our culture; it serves a plethora of purposes, from celebrating special occasions, to enjoying a social atmosphere with friends, to dating, and beyond. The concept of being waited on; of having a quality meal brought from behind closed doors directly to the table, without any self-labor, is hugely enticing, and also wonderfully mysterious. However, it is in that same mystery that certain problems can arise. One must be extremely careful when ordering a meal at a dining establishment. Not only is it important to understand the relative nutrition of the plates ordered, but now it is also equally vital to gain knowledge regarding the origins of the ingredients. Unfortunately, this information can prove extremely difficult to come by. Taking these notions into account in my own recent dining experiences and subsequent research, I discovered that many restaurants do an inadequate job—some perhaps intentionally—at providing the proper information of their ingredient suppliers to their potential customers, creating an unfortunate ethical dilemma for all those who chose to eat out.

The date is Tuesday, June 5th, 2012. I am rummaging through my pathetically bare cupboards in an attempt to conjure up some dinner for myself, when my two roommates enter the apartment and suggest we go out for dinner tonight. He mentions that the popular chain Buffalo Wild Wings has a special on Tuesday evenings, in which customers can get buffalo-style chicken wings, for which the chain is known, for fifty cents apiece. I'm game. We walk downstairs and into the dining area (my apartment exists in the same building as the Buffalo Wild Wings, a big factor in this being our restaurant of choice), and take a seat in a booth adjacent to one of the most gratuitously massive flat-screen televisions I have even seen, broadcasting a Detroit Tigers game. The three of us agree to take the "when in Rome" approach; that if we are going to eat here, we should fully immerse ourselves in the mythos of a "B-Dubs" dining experience . . . by ordering sixty wings, prepared with various flavored sauces, ranging from the relatively innocuous "honey-barbeque" to the painfully spicy "blazin'," and many in-between flavors on the spice continuum. Our order arrives as six small mountains of chicken, coupled with a single plate of celery that is dwarfed in comparison.

Thirty minutes and twenty wings each later, my lips and mouth are on fire, I have multiple sauces smeared across my face and hands, my eyes and nose are running uncontrollably, my stomach is churning from in intense amount of acidity I just imbibed, and I'm starting to feel a headache coming on. I feel like the most unattractive possible version of a human being. This is not to say that my meal was not a positive experience; quite the contrary, actually. Each wing was deliciously bold with flavor, and there is something inherently fun about the act of eating wings that should not be understated. It is, however, safe to say that this may have been the most physically taxing process required to enjoy good-tasting food that I have ever encountered.

It was only after the fact that I was reminded of my responsibilities toward understanding just what I was eating. As the waiter returned to retrieve our demolished plates, I asked him where the establishment got their chicken supply. He looked initially confused, and then concerned. Finally, after a few-second pause, he responded inquisitively, "I'm sorry, was there a problem with your meal, sir?" I quickly alleviated his worries; letting him know that I was just curious about the origins of the food I consume. He politely admitted that he was unsure, but could find out by asking a manager before leaving our presence. When he returned, several minutes later with the check, he apologized and said, "I'm sorry, I don't have the information you asked about." I paid the bill and walked back up to my apartment, suddenly a tad unnerved. To me, there were one of two likely possibilities, and neither offered a particularly appealing realization. The first possibility is that the manager he asked also didn't know where their chicken was coming from, which, depending on the rank of the manager, could have possibly been acceptable. The second possibility contains a much more problematic scenario: was it possible that the manager did, indeed, know the restaurant's meat supplier, but consciously chose not to have that information disclosed to a customer? I shuddered at the thought, and had a particularly restless night of sleep.

Obviously, it would be foolish to condemn the integrity of the entire Buffalo Wild Wings franchise on assumption. And, even if my conjecture was true, and the manager did knowingly refuse information about the business's meat supplier(s) to me, that still only represents *one* manager at *one* of the over 800 total restaurant locations, and is not necessarily a reflection of the franchise's viewpoints or business tactics. However, upon further digging, it became increasingly apparent that Buffalo Wild Wings is actually very reluctant to share its meat supplier information with its customers.

A trip to the company's website proves to be a powerful visual stimulus; the home page is a giant interactive half-football field, half dinner-table, stocked with various cued sound effects and animated icons that link to a variety of different sub-sites. There is a store locator powered by Google Maps, an interactive pop-up menu, a link to an electronic merchandise store, where apparel and gift cards can be purchased, a section for downloadable smart-phone apps, and a slew of wing-themed webgames, for starters. What they do *not* have, on the other hand, is any nutritional information, nor any names of ingredient suppliers. On the FAQ page, they do offer an external PDF file that lists the nutritional information, but this document is only available to those that take the time to fill out a fairly extensive comment feedback document, which requires one to provide his or her name, address, phone number, email address, the location of the restaurant the customer last ate at, a series of ratings of different aspects of the dining experience, and a short essay of comments, explaining the reasoning behind filling out a comment application, plus a written request for a document of nutritional information. In my comment application, I asked for a nutritional information PDF as well as any information the franchise had in regards to their chicken suppliers, specifically for the Ann Arbor location, if possible.

Roughly fifteen minutes after sending this request, I received a response from Buffalo Wild Wings, thanking me for my feedback, and promising a timely answer to my questions. Forty-eight hours later, I finally had my hands on the document of nutrition information, which I found to have not been updated since the year 2009. I was not surprised to discover that I had consumed roughly 1500 calories at my B-Dubs dinner, something that, though completely excessive, I could live with. On the other hand, the supplier information was totally absent from this email; I apparently had to continue to wait patiently for the information I actually wanted. It has now been two full weeks since I sent out the email requesting said information, and still I am waiting. I am beginning to think they're not going to respond.

Every minute that has passed since eating those delicious wings; every additional failure to find the information I am looking for made the task of finding the Buffalo Wild Wings chicken supplier information seem less like a research project and more like an investigation. Scouring the far regions of the web, no tangible answer to my question could be found. I quickly realized that I was not the only one who was looking for these answers. Dozens, possibly hundreds of blog and forum posts were devoted to discovering where B-Dubs got their chicken from. Each post shared a common theme: nobody had a legitimate answer. There were even claimed instances of these bloggers contacting the BWW customer support hotline, and asking a live representative where the restaurant gets their meat products. None were given an answer. Obviously, anyone can write anything on the internet, and the views of a single individual are not exactly the most credible source. But when hundreds of people reach the same conclusion, that nobody knows the answer to this single simple question, a pattern with seemingly zero exceptions arose. I felt as if we were all trying to uncover the mystery of the century, and whoever knew the answer was not about to give it away.

Clearly, this presents a huge problem for all of us. A vital step towards us being able to make dietary choices that reflect a sustainable and ethical means of obtaining food involves us having a firm understanding of that food. It's such an obvious notion; should we not have the privilege to know as many details as possible regarding a substance that we are trusting enough to put into our bodies? And, yet, in a startlingly high percentage of the food we order and eat, these details are not available to us.

What's interesting in this issue of non-transparency, is that the restaurants are only partially at fault. As consumers, every business, every single private entity attempting to sell us goods or services, is constantly adapting to our behaviors. Through careful observations of our desires and tendencies, businesses are perpetually striving to tailor to our needs and wants. Every action, every purchase, every piece of feedback, is considered, and is utilized in order to shape what the business emphasizes and values. This is the art of marketing. While businesses have been advertising their products for all of history—some scholars date the first advertisements back to 4000 B.C. (Bhatia, 2000)—the idea of marketing, that is, the creating, communicating, and exchanging of offerings that are believed to hold value for potential customers, is something fairly new, believed to have been developed in the mid-to-late 1940s (Shaw & Goodrich, 2005).

One thing that separates food from many other sold goods, however, is that it will never cease to be in high demand. While a particular style of apparel may go out of style over time, or piece of technology may be rendered obsolete, food is constant. We need to eat it—quite often—to maintain our health and continue to survive. It is postulated that these reasons have been a primary reason that, in general, overall perceptions of the qualities that consumers look for in their dining experience have remained roughly the same in the past half-century (Lewis). In general, as collected by survey, some of the main aspects of dining that consumers consider important are convenience, atmosphere, and taste (National Restaurant News). Multiple sources, including the aforementioned Lewis and NRN articles, have repeatedly found the most important factor consumers consider when choosing a restaurant is consistency. Consumers expect that if one experience at a food establishment is positive, that all subsequent trips to the same establishment will yield the same results. The founder of the application of this notion of perfect consistency was Ray Kroc, the man who developed the brand image of McDonald's, which now stands as the most recognizable food franchise on the planet. Kroc established the concept that no matter which of the hundreds of McDonald's restaurants a customer walked into, that he or she would be getting an identical product (Bannister, 2011). This has proven to be an immensely successful business model, as nearly all restaurant chains now attempt to achieve and maintain this uniformity.

However, while restaurants continue to strive for absolute consistency, one aspect of food that tends to be completely glossed over is food health, sanitation, and safety. The previously cited consumer surveys mentioned that while consumers do consider food safety to be a hugely important factor, it is also a general assumption that successful restaurants already inherently provide that, through strict legislative health standards and regulations. This consumer assumption gives restaurants the opportunity to scrape by on the bare minimum of emphasis on the true nature of the ingredients, should the intent to do so be present. In the Lewis article, it is suggested that for the last fifty years, restaurants have gotten away with recycling the same vague and generic statements regarding their food products; restaurants claim to use "wholesome," "top-quality," ingredients, claiming to hold the food they serve to the "highest standard," without ever defining what they mean by these statements, or offering any evidence to support these claims . . . and they get away with it.

The problem lies in the inability of many consumers to be able to critically analyze the claims the restaurants are making. In general, so much trust is placed in the restaurant to serve safe meals, that we allow the same restaurants to violate those trusts behind closed doors while emphasizing the importance of uniformity in our meals. Of eight different county health inspection reports (Hidalgo, Berkeley, Boone, McDonaugh, Fredricksburg, Montgomerey, Melbourne, and Chesterfield county health inspection) of various Buffalo Wild Wings locations throughout five states that I found while searching for the ever-elusive information regarding meat-suppliers, all eight locations were issued a Category I rating (or equivalent), signifying "high risk of foodborne illness."

And still, we consumers allow ourselves to be kept oblivious to the details of the food served to us because we overlook these issues in favor of concerns over consistency and uniformity of our products. When browsing the Buffalo Wild Wings website, one particular piece struck me as especially ironic. On the FAQ page, an entire paragraph was devoted to the apparently often-asked question, "Why are some wings larger than others?" I read this, and couldn't help but wonder why "Why does your franchise consistently rate so poorly when the risk of foodborne illness is assessed?" wasn't a question more frequently asked. The Center for Disease Control estimates that 76 million cases of foodborne illness occur annually, with 65% of cases coming from restaurants, and we are more busy worrying about the fact the set of wings placed in front of us aren't identical. Restaurants may be concealing truths about their food to us, but it's only because we let them through our ignorance. This problem is *our* fault.

Not all outlooks on this situation are bleak, however. The proper consumer action can be taken to change these restaurant practices into a more transparent atmosphere, and in some ways, is already trending in a positive direction. Web sources such as Real Time Farms offer maps that link restaurants to the farms that receive their products from (see Figure 1). This site currently lists fifteen participating restaurants in Ann Arbor alone that get their supplies from local organic sources. New restaurants that emphasize supplier transparency are also beginning to emerge. The Grange is a primary example of an Ann Arbor restaurant that promotes the farms that supply its ingredient both within the walls of the restaurant and on its innovative website, in which every ingredient served is hyperlinked to the farm it came from, merely a click away (see Figure 2).

Perhaps the biggest news of recent progress emerged this past January from one of the most unlikely sources. McDonald's, the reigning fast food juggernaut of the world, launched a transparency campaign entitled, "Field to Fork," which introduces McDonald's customers to the company's potato, lettuce, and beef suppliers, respectively, through a series of short informational videos. As of right now, McDonald's is the only major restaurant chain to have taken on such an extensive policy of transparency, but this new campaign offers a possible preview of a trend we may see seeing more of as consumer pressure increases.

In the end, it is up to us to demand a more transparent environment in the world of dining out if we expect positive strides to take place. We must vocalize our desires and opinions on these matters. We must inform our friends and acquaintances about the issues at stake. But most importantly, we must act. If you are planning on eating out, check the restaurant first, either by checking its website for ingredient supplier information, cross-referencing the establishment with Real Time Farms, or by calling and asking the restaurant where they are getting their ingredients. Beware of chain restaurants. If you must eat at a restaurant you have little information about, do not be shy to ask your waiter about where their ingredients are supplied from; if the waiter or manager cannot tell you the answer, try selecting a vegetarian option, and make a point to not return until you can find out more. And, of, course, don't forget to listen to your friends and family when they warm you not to eat somewhere with a lecture on "how bad" it is; they may know something you don't.

It is through our actions that we, as consumers, have the power to reshape the landscape of how businesses that offer their products to us conduct themselves. We must continue to emphasize our demands for more transparent food in the dining experience, putting pressure on eating establishments to accommodate these demands. Is it only then that we can guarantee the possibility of ordering a safer, more ethical dish. Then, perhaps, I can someday in the near future return to a Buffalo Wild Wings, and not only enjoy a plate of zesty wings, but also be equipped with the peace of mind of *knowing* my chicken, both the "what" and the "where."

Figure 1: Real Time Farms connects eatery to farm via an incredibly simple-to-use map interface. Check it out at http://www.realtimefarms.com/ the next time you're looking to go out for dinner.

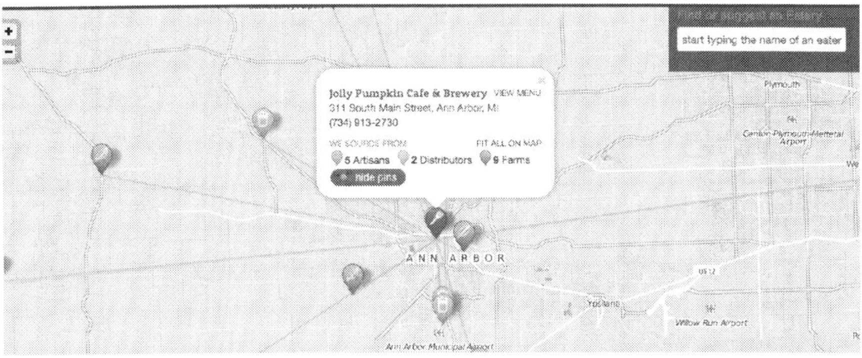

Figure 2: Ann Arbor's The Grange is a restaurant that prides itself in its locally sourced ingredients. Its electronic menu lists the name of its supplying farms as the visitor hovers his or her mouse over the ingredient in question. A simple click of the mouse takes the internet browser to that particular farm's webpage. http://grangekitchenandbar.com/menus.php

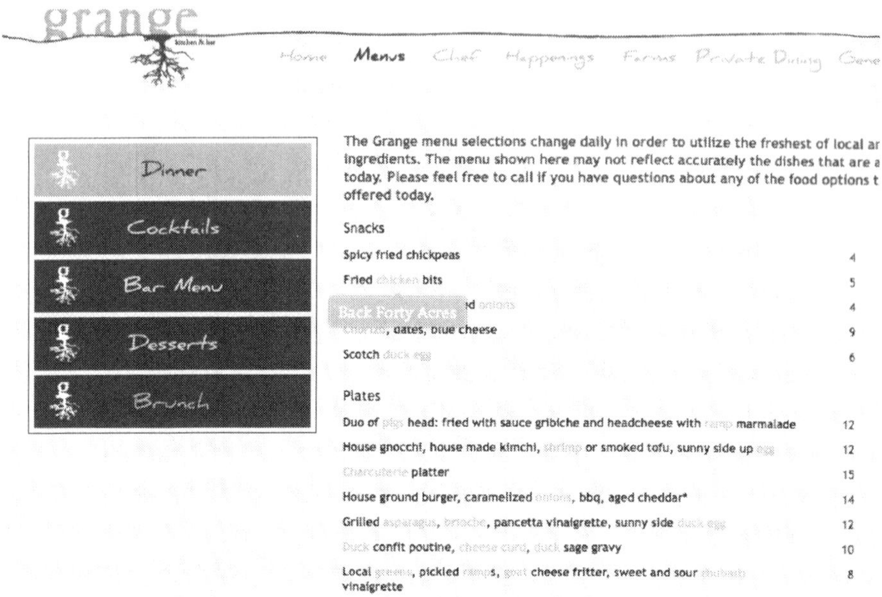

References

(2009-2012). In *Health Inspection Cases for Hidalgo, Berkely, Boone, McDonaugh, Fredricksburg, Montgomerey, Melbourne, and Chesterfield Counties*. Retrieved June 10, 2012

(2012). In *Buffalo Wild Wings Official Franchise Webpage*. Retrieved June 6, 2012, from http://www.buffalowildwings.com

Bhatia, T. (2000). *Advertising in rural India: language, communication, and consumerism* (pp. 60-68).

CDC estimates: prevention is key to avoiding foodborne illness outbreaks. (2007, May). In *U.S. Food and Drug Administration*. Retrieved June 13, 2012

Know Where Your Food Comes From. (2012). In *Real Time Farms*. Retrieved June 10, 2012, from http://www.realtimefarms.com/

Lewis, R. (1982, May). Restaurant advertising. *Cornell Hostipal Quarterly*, 23(1), 79-84. Retrieved June 10, 2012

McDonald's supplier stories: Always fresh from field to fork. (2012, January). In McDonald's Official Webpage . Retrieved June 11, 2012, from http://www.mcdonalds.com/us/en/supplierstories.html#/

Shaw, E. H., & Goodrich, K. (2005). Marketing strategy: from the history of a concept to the development of a conceptual framework [Electronic version]. , 265-270.

Targeting your demographic. (2012, April 30). *Nation Restaurant News*. Retrieved June 11, 2012, from http://nrn.com/article/targeting-your-demographic?as=independents

Bannister, A. (2011, June 13). Ray Kroc. . Retrieved June 15, 2012, from http://uk.businessesforsale.com/uk/F1644/mcdonalds-franchise/articles/McDonalds-franchise-Ray-Kroc

Matt Kelley Award for Excellence in First-Year Writing

First-year writing is a great leveler. It provides one of the few common spaces at the University of Michigan. Students cross paths with other students they're unlikely to encounter otherwise. Outside of the classroom they may separate into different academic and social groups, but inside the classroom, they exchange ideas, essays, and feedback. Irrespective of their background or academic interests, first-year writing pulls students together, and gives them a shared project.

The diversity of the first-year writing classroom is reflected in the range of student work instructors nominated for the Matt Kelley Award for Excellence in First-Year Writing. Students wrote engaged essays about everything from mathematics and Greek choruses to Star Wars and Starbucks. Time and again, their nominating instructors and judges praised students for their innovation, creativity, and originality.

This year's nominees for the Sweetland Prize for Outstanding Writing Portfolio demonstrated the wide-ranging perspectives and experiences that exemplify the joys and challenges of Writing 100 classes. Writing 100 students are asked to engage in deep reflection on their writing process—they consistently deliver in portfolios their readers described as delightful, distinctive, and perceptive.

We expect a great deal of first-year writers. In the midst of one of life's biggest transitions, we ask them to argue, analyze, and reflect in new academic contexts. We push them to develop new writing skills, and prepare them for impending academic rigors. They exceed our expectations in surprising ways. As a result, this year was a particularly challenging judging cycle. I am grateful to my colleagues who generously volunteered to serve as this year's judges: Scott Beal, Louis Cicciarelli, Tim Hedges, Jamie Jones, Dave Karcynski, Ray McDaniel, Christine Modey, Lila Naydan, Simone Sessolo, Naomi Silver, and Carol Tell.

We hope you enjoy these essays as much as we did, and that they offer you a glimpse into some of the tremendous talent and potential of our first-year students.

Dana Nichols
Lecturer, Sweetland Center for Writing

When the Silence Settles

From LHSP 125: Yardain Amron (nominated by Tim Hedges)

This essay tells a compelling story and relies on strong narrative instincts. Instead of just being a tale of a fight at a frat party, the essay digs deeply into issues of identity and the silences we create (and the silences we disrupt) in our daily lives. It is extremely well-written with an innovative structure, and it achieves a level of personal scrutiny not often seen in first-year writing.

Tim Hedges

When the Silence Settles

As we approach the frat-castle, my stained hands trace the black sharpie in my pocket—my voice, replaced by a two-dollar plastic tube filled with ink.

Up four termite-ridden stairs, we are stopped by a red Ralph-Lauren polo, collar fully popped, fitted like a wet suit. Beyond, an array of padded sweatshirts, leg warmers, and khaki shorts splashed in retro purples, teals, and pinks crowd the porch. They sip their red cups leisurely, enjoying the fresh air of a cool November night—an escape from the deafening bass leaking out from under the door.

"Who are you guys?" arms crossing condescendingly; I wait for the stressed stitching to snap and split the polo in two. I wonder how he landed the bouncer gig. Is he in an hourly rotation with the other brothers? Or is it a coveted position, won by the mightiest display of testosterone?

"I'm George. This is my friend Howard. He doesn't speak."

A pair of eyes locks onto my scrawny figure, noticeably taken aback, but trying to keep their cool. I stare back confidently, uselessly, silently.

Day 0: Tea for One

The idea was born in Sarah's room over cold tea. The tea guided our conversation to yoga, which progressed to yogi's in the Himalayas, my desire to study with one, and finally to silent retreats.

"…Yeah, my friend went on one once. She said it was pretty intense. No talking for a whole weekend and a lot of meditation." She pulls her legs up onto the chair, her chin coming to rest on her knee.

"That sounds awesome" I say. "Like no talking to anyone?"

"Yeah, you're basically supposed to explore yourself and I guess you do that best within your own mind."

"That's it!" I jump up from the bed, forgetting the bunk above and tea resting by my foot. Skull meets wood; tea meets carpet.

"Fuck!" I rub my head and scrunch my face. "A vow of silence! That's it." I barely notice Sarah anymore. I realize this idea has been steeping way longer than this tea.

Back in high school, parties took up a lot of my time, like a drug that only gave bad trips. They were my escape from seriousness. I could never resist. What if I missed that epic brawl? Better to get fucked up than watch *Bridezilla* marathons with Mom. I would find myself an hour deep in Brooklyn, already dreading the drunken subway ride back to the Upper West Side. Often I would pass out heading home and wake to the shake of an MTA employee. "You in the Bronx honey, best you find your way home." I began to see parties not as liberation, but as prison, the same monotonous drunk act over and over again.

I could spend my time more productively. I could stay home, read, write, play piano and study. I could enjoy and improve *myself.*

One night, I stumbled across a TED talk on YouTube by Susan Cain titled: "The Power of Introverts." I watched as she explained how introverts are looked down upon by society, how there is a bias within "our most important institutions, our schools and our workplaces. They are designed mostly for extroverts." Western culture shuns the recluse who prefers a book to a round of beers. I was mesmerized as she said, "some of our transformative leaders in history have been introverts;" Einstein, Gandhi and Beethoven, proof "Solitude is a crucial ingredient to creativity."

It's my last night with speech and I'm with Sarah—no tea this time.

I drop my bag and set the soft chocolate-chip cookie on the table. Sarah's face lights up.

"Thanks! I've been craving one since I started working." Her legs, propped up on a lime-green desk chair, fall to the ground as her hands grab the cookie.

The small study room is bright, a combination of LEDs above and gold carpet below. I pull up a chair opposite Sarah and heave my psych textbook from my bag to the table.

"I'm starting the vow tomorrow. I won't be talking to you for a week."

"Oh wow. Can I text you?"

"You can, I wont respond though."

"Well that's no fun…Email?"

I laugh. "Gonna miss me Sarah?" I say playfully.

"Maybe a little...A week's a long time. I'm not sure I would have the willpower." The rest of the cookie disappears into her mouth.

I think: *You don't need willpower when you want something.*

Day 1: Silence is Golden.

With 'CANT SPEAK' inscribed in black sharpie, my palm became my spokesperson. Everyone wanted more. "Why?" I shrug. "Are you sick?" Shrug. "Did you lose your voice?" I open my hands, shrug. "You're weird."

I notice all the small, insignificant interactions and courtesies. Someone holds the door, expecting a "Thank you." I walk through without looking back. In the elevator: "What floor?" I nod awkwardly and punch four myself. A text from Layne: "Dinner?" I eat alone.

Ordering required a mutual trust between server and myself.

"What would you like?" A cute blonde girl asks, mechanically grabbing a green plate from the colorful stack. Her yellow Michigan hat is fitted too tightly to her head. I want to tell her to loosen it. Her sincere eyes meet my nervous ones.

I point to the mashed potatoes like an infant; I imagine my mom: "Use your words Howard"

She looks hesitant. "Is he mute?" I picture her wondering. No, I just want some potatoes…

She plops a scant spoonful onto the plate.

Do I look that small? I'm a growing boy.

I slide my tray down the metallic counter weakly. What looks like sloppy-joe is next. I look for the label but it's missing from the holder. I stare at the mystery protein, look up at the girl and frown. How easy it would be to ask; three words: "Is that vegetarian?" I sigh and give her the thumbs up. She hands me the plate. I guess I'll settle for a salad.

Teeth brushed, I sit in the dorm hallway absorbed in my nightly journal. I flow without a filter, unlike my formal writing.

…What is the purpose? To simply not speak to anyone? Not interact. Or is it to avoid people?

George walks by in a towel, hair dripping. Bending down, he grabs my room key lying next to me and starts walking away. I laugh to myself. I jump up, letting my journal slide to the floor, and run after him. I grab his shoulder and try to snatch the key from his hand. His arms pull away.

"Woa. Use your words. What would you like?"

You bastard. You feel power over me. I'm weak…

I shake my head and try to snatch the key again. He pulls back.

He laughs mockingly. "You're like Jesus in the desert and I'm the devil. Here you go." He flicks the key to the floor and disappears into his room.

I pick up the key and head back to my journal, dejected.

…Ok so what is an improvement from today? Open up your ears! Don't speak. Listen. Silence is Golden.

Day 2: Clowns & Calculus

Wednesday passes quickly as I await a 6pm calculus exam. Finally, we are herded into the auditorium. Two girls at the front of the pack try to cram in that last equation. "Quick, explain the race-track principle one more time," "When do you use the Second Fundamental Theorem?" I yawn. Stress is your worst enemy going into an exam.

I find a seat in the back by the wall. My chair squeaks loudly as it swivels to create distance from the wooden table. The room is noisy, a blend of laughter and panic. I close my eyes and meditate for a minute.

"We will be handing out the exams now," a GSI announces from the front.

The room falls silent. Not a whisper. I try to sit still, hoping my chair's squeak won't disturb the beautiful silence. They have all lost their right to speak. We are all equal now, each of us restricted to our own minds. We are powerless—or is it powerful? I listen to the sound of paper slide on wood.

That night, as I try to pull Howard Roark from the pages of *The Fountainhead*, I get a knock on my door; three closed fist knocks: David. "I know you can't talk. Let's smoke."

With a J snug behind his ear, we make the long walk to the Arb. These walks are usually filled with passionate philosophical dialogue. We exchange ideas and opinions with little effort. We interrupt each other whenever there's the urge; as the idea enters the conscience, it exits the mouth, no delay. We have come to understand this as the best way, or comfortable way to converse.

But as we walk to the Arb this time, a new monologue emerges. David confides what I deem a deep secret; "she is the first and only girl I have ever loved." At times, I desperately want to interject; "*how do you know what love is*?" The words almost spill. I grunt instead.

We settle silently into our normal bench, overlooking an open field.

A blue light flashes at a relaxing pace under the distant skyline. A dog's howl echoes around us, as if we are in a cave. We feel powerful.

David lights the J and begins a new story about a poor boy named Timmy and a mean clown named Bobo. Now, I listen without an urge to reply. I listen because I enjoy David the storyteller. At the end, I want to tell him how talented he is, how impressed I am. I want to discuss the story, hear what he thinks the moral is.

But we walk home in silence. My own head is abuzz. I listen, feeling each thought pass through my conscience like sticky glue slowly sliding across my brain. This is flow. I am listening.

As the dorm comes into view, David breaks the silence. "I just want you to know that I wouldn't have told you any of that if you could talk."

Day 3: Slips and Sadness

My emblazoned palm is more than my spokesperson; it is my lifeline. As I head into psych lecture, a fresh phrase stains skin: 'I CAN LISTEN.' I find my regular lefty-desk in the 500-seat auditorium and pull up the lecture slides on my laptop: 'Development: Part 2.' David squeezes through the aisle and sinks into the seat next to me. The lights dim, a film flickers on before us: *Through a Child's Eyes: 9/11, an HBO Special.* The buzz in the auditorium drops to a hush. We are ready to listen.

Child after child tries to make sense of 9/11: "Why can't God stop the bad people?" six-year old Wajiha wonders; "I'm going to be a fireman when I grow older. Like my dad was," says little Shayne, decked out in a plastic firefighter costume. I sink into my seat. "It's like a mountain of sadness that gets smaller and smaller until it's just a little bump," says Katie who also lost her father. I sink deeper into my seat and close my eyes; I don't want to listen anymore. "I feel something good is coming. It just hasn't happened yet," a high, nasally voice says.

Wait. I know that voice.

I open my eyes to see a young Yedidya Schwartz, a kid I know as 'Didi.'

"What. I know that kid. That's Didi!" I blurt out.

David turns to me, astonished.

My upper lip eats my lower lip. *I just spoke... Oops.*

Day 4: God Speak

Thursday afternoons at 3:15, I debate God and religion with an orthodox rabbi on Hill Street. We have been at each other's throats for over two months now. Today won't be much of a debate.

As I lock my bike to the misplaced 'YIELD' sign in the front yard, I notice the 'Jewish Resource Center' banner hanging from the second floor balcony; without the sign, the neglected house would be mistaken for an abandoned shack.

Up three soggy steps, my shoes chip turquoise paint to reveal more naked wood. Inside, the house feels unstable, the floor almost hollow. I follow the narrow staircase to the second floor. At the top, my back slides down the wall until my butt finds floor, legs stretch out, and my torn Vans add prints to peeling wallpaper. I grab at my ears; headphones fall to my chest, dangling out from the top of my green windbreaker—my mom's from the 80's. I am early, as usual.

I listen to two young voices—one younger than the other—from an open door down the hall:

"...states children are not to suffer for their parent's sins. But Deuteronomy claims explicitly that children *shall* suffer for their parent's sins. Explain to me how that contradiction makes sense."

"I can point to hundreds of contradictions in the texts. Much better than the one you provide. I could go through each piece of text separately and explain the logic and context surrounding. But I believe you have a better question than that one, a bigger a question. But, our time is up. Think about it for next week."

A chair pushes back; a jacket zips; a bag thuds against a back. "Thank you rabbi."

I get up and hug the wall. A tall lengthy kid with a knitted Keepah on his head and Samba's on his feet appears from around the corner. He side-steps through the narrow passage, disappearing down the stairs with his head down. It has been four weeks and I have yet to see his eyes.

I enter. Rabbi Bausk sits behind a desk strewn with rabbinic texts; a naked mattress lies awkwardly on a metal bedframe to his right. His head is covered with his usual plain black Keepah. I smile and take a seat. I feel weak.

Bausk says: "I got your email. I'm more than happy doing all the talking. You realize I have you just where I want you. I could frustrate the bejeebers out of you. I'm so excited; I don't even know where to start. But I'll be nice to you."

He would rather listen to himself. Reinforce what he already believes as fact. That is our difference. I am here to listen, to question my own beliefs. He is here not to listen, but to reply and refute.

The next 45 minutes fly by. I listen as he explains the reasons behind the oral vs. written texts. "The written Torah is like the textbook. The oral Torah is like the lecture. The lecture keeps the interpretation of the textbook uniform. God wrote the book *and* gives the lecture..." Thoughts, questions, and arguments whizz down my pencil, filling my yellow legal pad: *'Power of speech,' 'Why do we desire uniformity?' 'This seems all too convenient.'* These points will make for a rich debate next week.

I leave the aesthetically neglected community house feeling intellectually nurtured. It was a new feeling compared to previous weeks. My passion and fear of being wrong usually deafens me. I become unable to listen, to see any sense in his beliefs. But today, I had been defenseless, unable to side with the comforting agnostic opposition. I listened deeper into the rabbi's words. Without speaking, I was composed, cool, and collected. My ears stayed open.

My desire to listen was greater than my desire to reply.

That night, I settle into my hallway alcove to journal.

Speech is an overused tool. Abused freely, it's my biggest weakness. Others can interpret my thoughts and tone and discover my vulnerabilities with ease.

Used thoughtfully and sparingly, my words are powerful, impressive, and desired. So listen first. Respond second. Remember, there are times to speak, and more times to listen.

Day 5, Part 1: Alone With Friends

It's Saturday night and I'm drinking beers with closed lips in David's room. Kendrick Lamar drowns out two conversations around me. Oregon vs. Oregon State is muted on the TV. My new friends surround me. I feel alone, frustrated, and tipsy.

"You alright?" David says.

Andrea and Sarah give me worried looks.

"He's alone in his world of the verb less" George fails with his eloquence.

I worry to myself:

Do I look that bad? Cheer up! Or at least don't show your loneliness. That's weakness.

I squint and nod assuredly at David. He looks unconvinced.

The Natty Lite cans that line the table lead the conversation to the economics of recycling. George's Clockwork Orange t-shirt ignites a debate over whether the book or movie is better. Sarah recalls the time a stranger convinced her to snort Adderall at a pregame. I listen, entertained.

"I miss his voice." Sarah makes a puppy face at me.

"That's crazy. I can't remember what it sounds like," David says.

"Me neither," George says. "What do you say we all put in ten dollars and make him not speak for another month?"

"No way, I miss Howard," Sarah says.

I'm right here. Aren't I…?

George pulls a Guinness from the mini fridge. I point at the beer and back at myself, twice. Without hesitation, he pulls another bottle and tosses it underhand. The wet glass connects with my hand like a baseball to a glove. Condensation spreads over my palm, sharpie bleeds from 'LISTEN.' My leg taps anxiously. How long has it been doing that? I grab a flip-flop from between my feet, pushing heel to bottle-cap confidently. I watch the cap launch like a rock from a catapult, disappearing over the TV. Should I get that? I stay seated.

My leg is still tapping. I continue a tantalizing thought:

Face your fear. Get with a girl at a party without saying a word. But whom would you be doing that for? For her? Definitely not. For your friends? I hope not. For you? Yes. Without your words, all you are is a cute face with some peach fuzz.

I jump up grabbing my coat from under me. My arms find holes, my fingers find metal and my eyes find George's. I point at the door.

Day 5, Part 2: Brothers & Bros

"And who do you know here?" The red polo turns to George.

George hesitates. "uhh, Brandon."

"Brandon who?"

George shrugs. "He's in our English class."

"Aight boys. I'm not trying to be a dick but you're gonna have to step off the porch and get outta here."

I'm not listening. I reach my right hand into slim khakis; my thumb and index maneuver around my wallet for my black sharpie—a fat one, a few hours old. My hand scribbles on my stained palm. I feel four eyes staring. I stretch my hand to his face. 'UR NOT TRYING 2 BE A DICK?'

My body's light; the balls of my feet press into the ground, ready to jump. I watch his hand, waiting for his fingers to curl into a fist. What am I thinking? The kid has at least 30 pounds on me.

"What are you doing?" He shakes his head, confused. "Just get outta here."

"We just want to party with you guys," George says pathetically.

An arm hooks around my shoulder, another around George's—Brandon, our hero.

"Yo B-dog, you know these kids?"

"Yeah, they're cool." Brandon grins widely, reveling in his new power and popularity.

"Ok B-dog, as long as you say so."

The brother-pledge class relationship confuses me: 'I can disrespect you when no one is around but at parties, we are tight.'

The polo steps aside and I pass quickly through. The front door is modern with a heavy-duty metal frame, maybe a response to the numerous home invasions plaguing campus lately. A rosy-cheeked brunette tumbles onto the porch, pigtails whipping my face as she jerks her head. I grab the door, and step up onto hardwood. I made it.

A narrow hallway packed with bodies and plastic cups. My ears throb in rhythm to DMX.

The dance floor is a good place to start, no words necessary, only hips.

I take a step but a hand suddenly pulls the back of my coat. I'm back on the porch.

A lengthy toothpick stands two inches taller than me, fake bling hanging stupidly on top of an oversized NBA jersey, plastic sunglasses hiding his insecurities. "Who are you? This is a themed party."

I shrug uselessly and point back at the red polo.

"He let us in." George is by my side again.

"I don't give a shit. You boys aren't dressed to theme. Get out of here."

It seems we have reached the next chain of command.

"Why does that matter?"

"Cause I say it matters. Did you hear me? Leave."

We aren't listening.

The door swings open again. A new pair of venomous eyes lock with mine. I feel his anger. The ringleader has arrived.

"What's the problem here? Who the fuck is this kid? Get the fuck out of here."

Everything falls away. His fury is unexplainable. He has no idea what has already happened. I have no idea what is about to happen.

George is explaining his case to the red polo. I take my sharpie and scribble on the back of my hand, above my thumb: "Y U SO MAD?"

His eyes jump from my hand to my face. "What the fuck are you doing?" His eyes beam at mine. Such anger. I stare back, unfazed. *Really, why are you so mad?* I'm back on the balls of my feet.

I watch him maneuver around the porch, sliding between unassuming leg warmers and polos. I watch his eyes lock on George, face contract, fist clench and without hesitation, arm swing. No remorse.

I need to yell, warn George who is blind to the impending fist headed for his face. I need to do something. I open my mouth to scream but no sound comes out. I am frozen.

Knuckles connect with George's left cheek; the sound is foreign, unlike the punches you hear in movie fight scenes, He drops to the ground, head slamming into concrete. I blink, stretching my eye sockets as wide as possible.

You drunk fuck. You couldn't even punch the right guy.

I jump towards him ready to draw blood. The red polo restrains my lean arms; hands lock around my biceps like handcuffs. I'm pathetic.

George props himself back on his feet, stunned.

"What the fucks his problem." George dabs his swelling lip gently.

I try to take a deep breath. We are outnumbered, outsized, and on their turf. I pull George by the arm and lead him down the stairs.

Back on the sidewalk, I slap my hand to my forehead, letting it slide down to my mouth. I jump in frustration. I clench my fists, pound my chest, and bite my lower lip. I want to scream.

I look at George and pound my chest three times with an open hand.

"The punch was for you?"

I nod.

"Did you provoke him?"

I put my thumb and index out, separating them by a small space.

"A little. Did I deserve it?"

I shake my head.

Guilt is overwhelming. My emotions are begging to be released.

I froze. I could have warned him…I choked.

I stare at the frat house in front of me. Fingers claim my belt buckle, unbutton my khakis, and pull my dick out. I piss on their lawn pathetically.

"That seems fitting. Did I deserve it?"

I shake my head again. We head back towards the dorm.

"Where were we earlier?"

I look at George worriedly.

"You haven't been speaking. I feel weird. I think I'm concussed."

Oh shit. I caused this. It's my fault.

"Did I deserve it? Do I keep saying that?"

I nod. I don't know what to do.

"What happened? Who were we with earlier…*did I deserve it?*"

I shake my head. I've heard enough. My ears turn inward.

OK easy decision. Hospital. Anything could be wrong. Don't think the worst yet. Stay in the present. Keep listening. Initiative.

I strike my arm in a north, then west direction—towards the hospital. My pace quickens; George follows.

He looks clueless. "I got punched. I've never been punched before. This is interesting."

I try my sharpie. My hand is completely stained. I pull up my sleeve and scrawl 'THINK ABOUT ANYTHING.' George stops and grabs my arm. He leans in, straining his eyes. His nose exhales on my skin.

"It's too dark. Why are you writing on yourself?"

Shit. He needs help now. This can't wait. He's lost in his own mind. What's your stupid vow of silence compared to a friend in need.

"George, what's the last thing we did in English class?"

" the...*Mother Night* trial?"

"Yeah. Tell me something about the trial"

"It ended, what two days ago? You were...I think you were Werner Noth. "

I quicken pace again; George adjusts.

"Is that right?"

"Not exactly." The trial ended a week and a half ago. I played Howard Campbell.

"Did I deserve it? Who punched me? You weren't talking before."

"George I need you to forget what happened. Forget tonight. Tell me about your brother."

I pretended to listen, my own thoughts directing my attention inward.

I just broke the vow. I failed. Yogis go their whole lives. I couldn't even last a week. No, don't think about it like that. Speaking was necessary. Listening was finally not enough. It took five days, but I finally needed my voice.

Day 6: Beneath the Silence

I woke up the next morning unsure George would know what year it is. I found him in the bathroom staring at the mirror.

"Hey check this out," thumbs curling over his upper lip, uncovering a blend of blues, purples and reds.

"Haha. Nice man. Do you know what day it is?"

"Yeah…Sunday. I couldn't remember that?"

"Naw, you narrowed it down to the weekend but couldn't decide on the day."

"Wow, what else happened?"

I told him the details. He had no recollection of talking with the police, The CAT scan, or even his obese doctor that I mistook for a grizzly bear. I watched his eyes expand as I explained how he kept reading his texts over and over again like a broken record, eerily repeating, "It's like I'm coming into someone else's life."

"Damn. That's scary. You must have been freaking out."

"Yeah, I was pretty worried. You feel fine now?"

"Yeah, I'm good. Did I deserve it?"

Oh god.

George bursts out laughing. "You should have just seen your face."

Relief floods my body, like the deep breath after the doctor tells you that lump in your neck is just a swollen lymph node. My fist connects playfully with his arm.

Word spread quickly around the dorm; I guess George was curling his lip like a trophy. But everyone wanted to hear a good story and George couldn't provide much detail.

At dinner, David finds me over a heaping plate of potatoes.

"I want to hear what happened from *you.*"

I tell a tale about two poor boys and a mean red polo. David listens.

I am the storyteller right now.

That evening, I head to yoga for a candle-lit class. As I climb the steps to the second floor studio, the peaceful humidity fogs my glasses. I look up to a blurred smile behind the haze—Jason, my instructor welcoming me in. Shoes and socks off, my feet exhale onto the smooth hardwood floor. The muted orange hue emanating from candles lining the room blends with the baby blue walls—a sunset.

I unroll my mat and find a comforting lotus position alongside my peers. My eyes flutter closed.

I follow Jason's voice as it travels from behind me and settles at the front of the room; he begins with same mantra: "Watch your breath. If your mind drifts away, bring it back slowly. To still the mind is yoga. *Listen.*" I have heard these same sentences for the past three months; today is the first time I listen.

A silence settles over the room.

In through the nose...My lungs expand and fill with life; I watch this life travel down my spine to my toes. Out through the nose...My chest slowly falls; the life is guided out of my nostrils.

Pure silence is nonexistent. There will always be my breath.

Thought leaves my mind blank. I listen to my breath, the breath around me. The sound of tires on pavement rushes by below. I listen. The muted laughter and clink of glasses seeps through the ceiling from the pub below. I listen. The energy within the room engulfs me and flows through me. I listen.

Breathe in...Breathe out...in...out...in...

Ink

From LHSP 125: Amelia Brown (nominated by Tim Hedges)

On the surface, this is a compelling narrative about getting a tattoo. However, the writer works hard to derive meaning from the experience and uses the essay to explore her own beliefs and values. She effectively frames the story around the idea of "permanence," and she presents well-paced and highly detailed scenes that move the reader smoothly through time. She does what good writers can do: she takes an experience that was meaningful to HER and she tells her story in such a way that it becomes meaningful to US.

Tim Hedges

Ink

Lounging in the fabricated warmth of the small and somehow cozy classroom, I slowly cracked each one of my knuckles before pulling my sweater sleeves back over my hands and leaning back in my hard metal chair. I rhythmically tapped my foot on the carpeted ground, a dull thudding noise persisting over the muted mumblings of my senior-year classmates. The question had been posed, "if you had to get a tattoo, what would you get, and why?" We played this game at the beginning of each class and as a study break when our minds, as assessed by our teacher, became too full to retain any more AP Government facts or PowerPoint slides. One of us would ask a question about any aspect of life, granted it was "school appropriate," and each member of the class would have to respond. Today's question was brought to the class by my acquaintance Lillian, who had clearly asked the "hypothetical" question simply to illuminate the class on her own current state of inkage, as she was one of the few high school kids that had a tattoo already.

I zoned out, listening to the sounds of Lillian's voice juxtaposed over the insect-like humming of the fluorescent lights, and waited for a clear cut image of dark ink forming some shape on my body. Several other classmates gradually replaced Lillian's voice, each answer resounding louder and louder as the student responding drew closer and closer to my seat. The speed at which my foot was tapping increased with the inevitable need for an answer to occur to me, and although this was surely not a life or death situation, my palms begin to sweat, urging me to release them from the death grasp I was holding them in on my desk top. "And what about you, Amelia?" my teacher chirped, lurching me out of the mental scramble I was trying to find order in. "Honestly, I have never really thought about it before," I mumbled. "Maybe a picture of the Giving Tree, from that Shel Silverstein book…up my leg maybe? I don't know." I raised one eyebrow and shrugged as my sentence trailed off and I began to doubt the actual aesthetic value of what I had just said. To be honest, I was not even sure what the Giving Tree drawing looked like, and was pretty positive it had never meant anything profound to me. I don't know what had inspired me to say what had word vomited out of my mouth, but the rest of the class and my teacher bought it. Several classmates nodded pensively, as if acknowledging a deep pool of value in which my answer floated, though personally I knew my answer was complete crap.

The rest of the responses went similarly, with each individual either staring back at our teacher in bewilderment, or attempting to pass off some last minute idea as a personal statement that had been years in the making, and was sure to find its way somewhere on their body within the next week or so. As I had taken a stab at that method myself, I was not fooled, and began to wonder what each person sitting in this room with me would actually get infused into their skin if time to contemplate was added and inhibitions were taken away. I looked at my friend Mason and saw his varsity football jersey number in thick, industrial letters on his back. My gaze strayed towards Anna, who drew on herself every day with permanent marker and would surely create a beautiful and whimsical doodle to solidify on the inside of her arm, or behind her ear. Then to my teacher, who was rumored to have a tattoo, which assembled itself in the form of a dragonfly or Chinese caricatures in my mind. And finally back to me. If my theory was correct that more time and the absence of hang-ups would allow me to permanently mark up my body, then what would I really get? Surely not an image from one of the most depressing children's books I had ever read, that somehow managed to scar me enough to become an on-the-spot classroom answer from somewhere in my subconscious. The question gnawed at me, eating me alive for a reason currently indefinable. I breathed deeply and resumed my calm exterior, pulling my sleeves over my damp hands once more and leaning back in my seat. Suddenly, a reason for the tension revealed itself: my inability to pinpoint what I would get as a tattoo inadvertently indicated a lack of knowledge about myself. I did not seem to know what was most important to me, and certainly couldn't determine what I was committed to enough to declare permanency. This plagued me. I had always considered myself to be grounded, in touch with who I am as a person, and easily able to describe my essence of being to those who bothered to ask. Yet in this moment, all of that toppled down from the secure pedestal it had once inhabited. There was a part of me that was unexplored, unanswered, and unsure. To this day, I still remember this sinking, hollow realization that swept over me in response to the most simple of questions.

Nearly a year later, the subconscious presence of the tattoo finally presented a feasible physical manifestation. I had been folding over the layers of this endeavor in my mind for weeks. I had tried to locate all the areas in which this could go terribly wrong and, as my stomach began to churn, settled instead on accepting whatever occurred in the following hour. After all, it was to be an experience. If anything went wrong, so be it. With this notion set in stone, I had zipped up my boots, walked out of Lloyd Hall, and stuffed my hands into my coat pockets, briskly stepping out to meet the cold rush of night air one last time as an unmarked individual.

I was surprisingly collected about this adventure, and had been for most of the anticipation of it. When my writing professor had requested us to "experience" something out of our comfort zone, it had instantly pulled that moment in my high school classroom out of my subconscious, and had given me the clear opportunity to finally discover what was permanent to me by getting a tattoo. I was excited to take advantage of my instructions, as I knew they would push me just enough to search myself and then make a commitment that I would not otherwise. Naturally, there was also the constant nagging in my mind that my parents would not support my tattoo. My mother, who I had casually asked over the phone several days before my appointment just to test the waters, had said that tattoos were "undeniably white trash, and that's not just a generational difference." My dad, who I had done the same to, had sighed and replied "I just don't understand why naturally attractive people want to mess all that up by permanently scarring their body. I have always said that tattoo removal is the next big business." The pain, the permanence, the consequences, all of these things had occurred to me and caused me to nearly call and cancel my appointment several times. Yet each time I came to the realization that this was for me, and my decision did not involve anyone beyond that. It may sound selfish, but I view it as the truth. To me, this experience presented the opportunity to take ownership of my body and soul and commit to myself and my life in a way I had not before. The very essence of my tattoo, a line from my favorite Anis Mojgani poem, would urge me to live each day as if it was my first and simultaneously my last. No matter what happened, I would be forced to accept the responsibility of shaking off the dead weight that can accumulate on a daily basis, and live to my fullest potential, as the words inscribed on my ribcage would not allow me to ignore this responsibility to myself. I would have to commit to choosing happiness, commit to keeping myself lifted, and commit to helping others do the same, permanently. After all this time since the confusion of that moment in my senior year, I realized that this was what was important to me: simply staying happy and living my life one day at a time, circumstances aside. Upon tying all of these thoughts together in a complete package of what this experience would mean to me, I fully concluded that none of the other aspects mattered. The pain, telling my parents, the monetary cost of nearly $150, all were irrelevant now. Yet still, not knowing exactly what I was getting into, this was to be an undeniably new and intriguing event in my life.

As I turned the corner onto State Street, the bright lights of downtown Ann Arbor hastened my focus from the blackened gum on the sidewalk to all that the night could offer me. An endless sea of black coats and bobbing hats passed me, and I breathed in the sharp air with confirmation that what I was about to do was right for me at this time in my life. I stepped into the street with purpose, and fixed my gaze upon the flickering neon signs beckoning from the second story window several shops down. "Tattoo," a pink sign palpably announced what was in store for me. My determined stride slowed as I reached the unmarked door, held slightly open by some faulty spring, welcoming me inside. I removed my gloves, finger by finger, pocketing them and clasping the cold metallic door handle with my bare hand. A flight of stairs led me to a dimly lit hallway with endless unmarked brown doors, boldly contrasted by a single glass door at the end of the hall. The glass door radiated neon lights that bounced off the checkered tile floor visible from my spot on the dull brown carpet. I made my way to the end of the hall, opening the door to the surprise of four thoroughly inked men sitting on a black leather couch. In their slight haze and the time it took them to realize who I must be, I took in the strangely calming room that surrounded me. The checkered tile floor gave way to a single glass table littered with magazines, a tattooed woman in a bikini on nearly every cover. The larger versions of these women were pasted on the walls around me, to such an extent that I could hardly discern between posters and wallpaper. One pinup styled woman looked down at me from on top of a car, her ribcage displaying a more extensive version of what I was sure my own would resemble in not too long. Underneath her gaze was a desk and a glass case of tattoo aftercare products, dully lit from below to remind me where to stop once my skin was sufficiently marked.

My assessment being complete, I turned back to smile at the men, one of which were now standing. "You must be Amelia," he said, to which I nodded and walked further into the room, sure that I did not end up here on accident and was in fact getting a tattoo. A man of few words, Johnny, my soon-to-be tattoo artist, stretched his dark ink-covered arms as he made his departure from the couch. I quickly scanned him over, taking in his the short black hair peeking out from a backwards "Obey" hat, his gauged ears, and his blank white cutoff shirt. My eyes caught a facial feature that I somehow had not noticed before; where I had thought I had seen two normal eyebrows, there was shaved skin tattooed so densely with a dark green design, that the ink eyebrows nearly looked real. I tried to process this quickly without Johnny catching me staring, and he did not seem to notice my temporary startled expression.

Following his relaxed stride, I was led into a room I had not seen at first. Tucked to the right of the main room, it was mostly bare save for a leather chair and various needles that lay out on a small metal table. Johnny handed me a stencil of the tattoo I had decided upon over email. "There's a mirror out in the main room, go hold it up to your body and tell me what you think," he said. My first inhibitions crept up as I processed the idea that I was supposed to go back into the room full of tattooed men, pull up my shirt, and casually assess my potential tattoo in the mirror without feeling the slightest bit odd. Decidedly in too deep to turn back, I walked out into the main room and followed Johnny's instructions. My ribcage received five stares: a nervous and unfocused one from me, and four hazy but interested gazes from the men still sitting on the couch. As I stared back at my own skin, aware of the eyes on me, I suddenly felt relaxation and awareness melt down my entire body. I wasn't sure if it was the low neon lighting, the quiet but insistent Tupac playing from a location unknown, or the knowledge that I was about to do something fairly risky by my own choice, but I slowly regained the same assuredness I had possessed on my walk here. This time, though, I also embraced a hint of danger. I felt empowered, in control, edgy, and slowly strode back into the room. I was not sure if I should be trusting Johnny, this man who I hardly knew, with my body. I was pretty sure he was stoned in fact. But lying down on the table, I exhaled and slipped into a deep calm anyways as I waited for him to turn the stencil in my hands into a finished product.

The needle bit into my ribcage and sent an electrical buzz up the entirety of my spinal chord. Johnny had warned me in his dragging, monotonous rumble of a voice that "it was going to feel a little cold," which now seemed to be the least accurate representation of what this actually felt like. I ran my nails down the length of the leather chair I was laying on, and made small, temporary dents in the chair's exterior when the needle most directly made contact with my bones. Johnny never talked, and made it clear that I was not allowed to either, as any movement in my ribcage could result in a slip of the needle. As I lay on my side, eyes closed, breath shallow, I let the methodic buzzing of the needle consume my mind. It was odd; I had been expecting the very worst. On every occasion that I had mentioned to someone I was getting a tattoo their response had been "good luck with that, I have heard the rib cage tattoos hurt like hell." I had prepared myself for the inevitable blood and pain that would eventually pay off, but this was simple, easy, and even relaxing. The dull mechanical noise had represented a biting pain at first, but had quickly faded into a numb and persistent presence that actually felt quite nice. The sound of the needle took me instantly back to the buzzing fluorescent lights of my high school classroom, the very first time I had contemplated being in this position. I would have never expected, sitting in that chair and contemplating what was most important to me, that I would be laying on a table with a needle in my side a year later, perfectly calm. If anything, the greatest tension that I felt in this moment was sexual, as lying on a table with my shirt off and a strange man running a needle over my bare skin was a type of physical contact I have never experienced before. Johnny was intriguing, and in the few words we did exchange his voice felt similar to the prick of the needle, and just as strangely soothing. Naturally, I wasn't planning on expressing any of these thoughts to him, as hitting on my tattoo artist was not on my to do list that night, but I couldn't help melting into his hand a little as he traced the words I had chosen into my side. All too soon, the musings of the friendly needle came to a halt; I felt a cold cloth wipe down my side, and Johnny's nearly inaudible, "alright, that's it." Shockingly painless and strangely pleasant, it was over. Yet all of the feelings I had accumulated lingered past the final buzz of the needle. I slowly sat up in a daze, rose from the table, and made my way back to the mirror. With still surrender my eyes greeted the reflection of my ribcage. "Shake the dust," it now read in typewriter font. The experience was complete.

The preparation for my tattoo, in all of my speculations about how it would feel, how my family would react, and if it would look as I had hoped, kept me awake at night. Yet in the moment, in the actual physical process of getting my tattoo, everything was calm. This perfectly reflected what I had hoped the experience would bring to me emotionally. I wanted to make this promise of permanence to myself, and the fact that the experience went off without a hitch confirmed my belief that it was the right thing to do and perhaps was even intended to happen. In following through with this experience, I was able to answer the question I could not for the previous year and a half; I knew what was permanent in my life. I learned, through the anxiety, the pain, and the pleasure, that what I most valued was "shaking the dust" off of my life. The needle has signed my contract, making a permanent promise to myself to live my life, shaking it by its clothespins, walking into it, breathing it in, and reveling in every moment it can offer me.

Sweetland Prize for Outstanding Writing Portfolio

Trishanya Raju

From Writing 100 (nominated by Paul Barron)

This portfolio is indeed outstanding. Not only is it visually appealing, the writing within satisfies the expectations set up by these visual elements. Throughout there's a love of language, a wealth of original thinking, and a careful attention to design.

A glance down the menu reveals a list of interesting titles, which deliver on their promises. These titles are specific because the essays have been carefully considered and are the result of significant revision.

Visually, the pages are balanced, the images well placed and well chosen. I particular like tha the images seem to purposefully co-ordinate with colors of the theme and the font. When I pointed this out to Trishanya, she mentioned that this was a conscious choice.

In the writing the voice is assured and research is integrated in such a way that it becomes itself a place for exploration, a way forward. I've read many student essays on affirmative action, and many on reverse discrimination, but "Trust Us, We Know Progress" is carefully argued and allows me to see this topic with fresh eyes. Likewise "Conforming to Anticonformity" distinguishes itself by its clarity of thought.

You can tell Trishanya really enjoyed working on this portfolio of writing. The smartness of her design choices reflect the smartness of the writing.

Paul Barron

Confessions of a Sci-Fi Junkie

When you think of a club, or group, that you are a part of, you are basically looking inside of this little box you have, called your 'Identity', for the little labels in it, which all form a part of you. Anything you associate yourself with, and everything you believe yourself to be is in that box. These little labels all form communities that you are a part of. However, some of these communities define your identity more than others do. These labels I imagine as being bright red, in contrast to the beige labels of your less defining elements. If I were to consider these beige labels, there are so many different communities that I could identify myself with. I could be a part of the community of "Indians" or "International Students." The pinker labels would have me claiming that I could be a part of the "musician" or the "writer" communities. There is no dearth of groups I could associate myself with after deconstructing my identity, but perhaps the one I've chosen is a community that shapes my identity the most, one of the brightest reds in my little box of labels. I'm a part of the community of Sci-Fi junkies, or maybe the term 'geek' would be better. I'm a geek.

Yes, it's true. I confess. I don't pretend to be a hard-core fan. I don't pretend to know everything about the worlds I love (no, I don't know Klingon or any forms of Elvish). I don't pretend to play the "REAL" videogames (no, I don't play Call of Duty or World of Warcraft). I play Crash Bandicoot, Dragon Ball Z and Midnight Club on the Play Station 2, but that doesn't make me any less a part of this community. No matter how far back in my life I think about, I have always been a geek. From trying to figure out how to reprogram our computer when I was 6, to spending hours playing Pokémon and quoting Sci-Fi movies to people who had no idea what I was talking about, when other girls my age had much rather played with Barbies (no doubt an influence on their current model for the ideal in fashion and appearance). I have to say that I was lucky; my family accepted me for who I am, though my mother often reproaches me for being the son she already has, in opposition to the daughter she thought she gave birth to. Science fiction, and my passion for it, has shaped my perceived identity. It's shaped the way I think and it's shaped the way I react to things. It's had such an impact on molding me that I should probably admit that my best college application essay was a Lord of the Rings themed poem about the Witch King of Angmar's (bad guy) defeat at the hands of Éowyn (good guy). It's because of science fiction that my dream was to become a fiction writer.

We geeks have no formal club, and we have no formal meetings. But we are together in our reverence for the genre of Science Fiction. We usually hide our passion, because the people we are friends with don't "get it," and we've learned to be quiet about it with them. We have the ability to blend in with the normal people, if we need to, because we mainly assemble online, and connect through soul stealing outlets such as 9gag (an unoriginal internet meme site like reddit). Before the Internet, only the lucky few geeks had found similar people to develop a sense of community with. With the rise of the Internet, however, geeks were among the first to create a vibrant virtual community. We have been transformed from an alienated and virtual community into a popular, real-world fraternity – and, to a lesser extent, a sorority – whose members are now able to interact physically, as never before. Even though we are divided into different subgroups, like the artists (those who enjoy drawing up their own comics), the comic book fans, the movie fans, the gamers, and the television show fans, these different factions all accept each other as part of a big happy, family.

Every geek has his or her own idiosyncrasies but I think that there are some that are universal. We have certain ways of doing things. The stereotype of geeks is that we are socially obtuse, that we aren't socially aware, and that we don't know how to be socially appropriate. It may be better to say that instead of being "uncool" we, or at least I, choose to reject the trappings of being "cool." We know that we are antisocial. We know that we are sometimes overly dramatic and have unrealistic expectations of things. We also know that some of us may not dress "fashionably" or talk using the latest "lingo" (seriously, YOLO?). We intentionally eschew the noticeable markers of cool by adopting or avoiding certain styles of clothes, topics of conversation, and ways of speaking so as to cultivate an identity and appearance of being different. Psychologist Mel Levine quotes "There are a lot of depressed cool kids, and it's better to be a happy geek than a popular anorexic…Geekiness isn't a pathology."

Moreover, it's not that we aren't social; it's more to do with the fact that our social interactions don't conform to the more traditional ones. I'll admit that sometime we can get a little carried away, and yes, we are borderline obsessive (be it with respect to movie/comic book releases, or mini action figure collections). But this is just our (slightly unrestrained) way of expressing our passion for all things sci-fi. Take Robin Williams, for example. A famous actor, Williams knew that he had to restrict himself to certain conventions, for the sake of his publicity, but he too realized his need for a sort of "geek outlet." To this end, he named his daughter Zelda, after Princess Zelda of The Legend of Zelda series of video games.

You may find yourself asking, then, "what's so great about being a geek? I don't reject being cool, and being obsessive about things doesn't sound like a good thing." To put it simply, science fiction has the potential to teach us the ways of the world. Take, for example, Spider-Man. To me, this was always about an awkward teenager finding his way in the world. Clearly, Stan Lee pasted his message on thick with the classic "with great power comes great responsibility." I believe that that also means behaviors have consequences. You learn to respect others and yourself. Even in Star Trek, you learn about war, race, friendship, and loyalty. You learn that the motivations behind people's actions aren't always black and white. People are complex and relationships are complex. McCoy and Spock (characters in the show) are always at odds, and yet they would lay their lives for each other. Isn't that what science fiction is about? What it means to be human? What it means to be alive in the world? How we face adversity and how we relate to other people in our lives. How we see ourselves?

Though the geek life may now sound attractive, our community does have its fill of awkward moments. I've begun to think of these moments as our "initiation" into the geek world. The moments I'm talking about are the embarrassing ones like when you wave your hand in front of your face and say "these aren't the droids you're looking for," or when you say "live long and prosper" instead of a traditional goodbye, and the reaction you receive is a group of blank stares in return. A moment of awkwardness. But then again, most moments of geek life are. Being a geek is in no way a life for the faint hearted. So in the end, what is a geek? Someone who likes cosplay or collecting comics? Someone who thinks aliens and spaceships are cool? Someone who wants to be just like Batman? Maybe, but we are also so much more. We are intelligent and educated, world-wise and well-rounded individuals. We understand ourselves and the world, and the people who inhabit it. I am what I am, and that's all that I am. So said Popeye, and I agree with him.

Conforming to Anticonformity

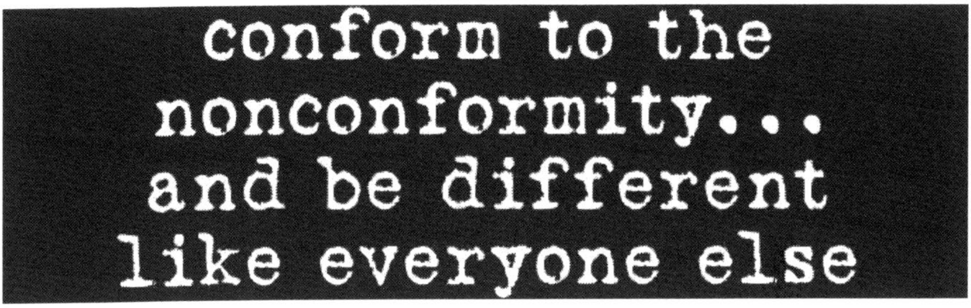

Be different, like everyone else.

> "If there is anything the nonconformist hates worse than a conformist, it's another nonconformist who doesn't conform to the prevailing standard of nonconformity." —Bill Vaughan

If you take one look around any metropolitan area, you see a horde of people each trying to be their own person. The people who are trying to make a fashion statement by wearing neon colored pants, or people trying to come off as metal fans by growing their hair out and wearing army pants. I say people, and not person because the screaming irony is that by trying to be different in the exact same way as everyone else, they actually are like everyone else.

Our need for conformity is nothing more than our desire to go along with the traditions or conventions of a group of people, in order to ensure that we will be accepted as a part of the group (instead of being rejected undesirable person or an outcast). Conforming to a group is a beacon signalling to members of the group that "I am like the rest of you. I follow our rules. I am not a threat." This signal indicates the consistency of behavior, allowing other people to be able to predict our actions. It is also a step along the journey to increasing our own credibility, or reputation within the group. However, people's need to be different is a contradiction to their need to be accepted. They want two things that are not likely to be attained as a package. Society would inherently reject anything that was an aberration. However now it would appear as though differences are celebrated rather than condemned. While a strong need to be different should cause people to be true to themselves, or rather, to be more original than their peers, the trend where a person is required to be different, or unique, to be accepted, might cause them instead to suppress their own desires and try to conform to "anticonformity."

"I'm not like most people" – most people

It doesn't have to be this way…

What is anticonformity? Anticonformity is deliberately going against established norms in order to appear to be different. It is more about acting contrary to the desires and expectations of others (norms) as a reaction to the others. This is in opposition to nonconformity, which is the refusal or failure to conform to accepted conventions, however it stems more from a person's true nature, rather than just the need to be different. It is no wonder that theorists and psychologists have wrestled with the idea of how people balance their need to be "included in social groups with their need to be different and distinctive." [1]

The strength of one's desire to conform is a quirk of one's personality, and as a result some people may try to conform to whatever group they are in at the time, while other 'anti-conformists' will go in the other direction. They may try to be deliberate in their assertions of their own individuality by rejecting all but a very few sets of norms, which they believe to be commonplace. However, rejecting everything that one perceives as popular is just as illogical as jumping on the wagon of every little trend that strikes up simply in action against the fear of "not fitting in." There are plently of directionless people who are so desperate, so in need of being nonconformists that they consecrate a great deal of their time to doing exactly the opposite of whatever "the masses" are doing, regardless of their own personal preferences. This form of "nonconformity" is more like what would be called "anticonformity," because we would not really doing what we want; but instead we would just be doing the opposite of what someone else wants. Not only is this practice pointless, it is also a huge waste of time. Whoever the anti-conformists are rebelling against -The Man, parents, America, the World in general – if they change their habits, the anti-conformists would have to change theirs. What they choose to wear, as well as what kind of music they listen to, has to change every time the "mainstream's" tastes and ideas about what the new "in thing" is, changes. Oh, everyone has a PC? Now we need to get a Mac. Macs

1 Hornsey, Matthew J, and Jolanda Jetten. n. page. Web. 18 Nov. 2012. <http://psr.sagepub.com/content/8/3/248.short

becoming the hot new thing? Time to go Linux. Every time something turns "mainstream," they have to have a change of lifestyle. The anti-conformists fall into the mainstream schedule, not their own. For instance, once upon a time, the minority considered all races to be equal. Now, however, that particular opinion is held by a majority of America. In keeping with the custom of anti-conformism, if the goal is to be a rebel and turn against the majority, theoretically, you would now have to start being a racist.

We all want to feel like we have some qualities that are worthy of notice, something that makes us stand out from the millions of other human beings spread out across the planet, especially now that it would appear as though the world has become and even smaller place, and the things that once set us apart as individuals no longer do so. There are no limits to the heights that some people are willing to climb in order to be recognized or established as different, and to simply be able to stand out in a crowd. But the thing is, the harder they strive to be different, the more they blend in with some particular subculture. And perhaps a clarification may be in order, I do not mean to suppose that all who adopt these preferences are necessarily doing it out of anti-conformity. It is definitely possible that there are several among those in the "clans" who are genuinely attracted to the lifestyles. However, I'm making a generalization based on the majority of my research. When, in my interviews, I asked people why they enjoyed a particular band or group that they had mentioned, they all replied that it was because, in essence, their friends did. Many of them replied to my question "why do you identify with the things/people you do?" with the answer "because no one else understands." I believe the problem lies more with the fact that instead of others not understanding them, they don't understand themselves, and they turn to what they believe they should associate themselves with; in order to give themselves some perceived identity, because they haven't been able to form one for themselves. This claim can be supported by the evidence of researchers who have found that people mainly with low self-esteem resort to anti-conformity.[2]

Every person is unique, and that means that the best way to stand out as different is to become the best possible version of yourself, even if that may mean that parts of you overlap with parts of someone else. Of course there may be parts that overlap, for example, you and a random stranger could like all the exact same music, however it is your other tastes that make you distinct. When your focus is on being you, instead of on being like someone else, there's no competition and no reason for comparisons. This is the essence of individuality. By chasing nonconformity as a means of being different, we are allowing "the flow" to direct our current. If they go left, we go right. If they go up, we go down. This is not individuality, it's simply contrarianism – a predictable response to the majority.

We all live our lives within a giant melting pot of borrowed ideas. Hardly anything these days can be considered original, without any pre-

---

2 "Social Psychology." <http://webspace.ship.edu/ambart/PSY_220/conformoutline.htm>

existing foundation, and our understanding of the world and ourselves is simply a mosaic of ideas that we've heard from other sources, things that we've picked up and patched over our existing collage of ideas along the way. We can always pick up new ideas and beliefs at any time, thereby shedding the old skin of what we no longer identify with. This is pretty much what growing up is all about. Change, becoming different people. I doubt most of us are the same people now that we were when we were, say, 5 years old. Our change is influenced by every single thing that exists already, be it stereotypes or the experiences of a friend. So yes, in a way, nothing is original. Nothing is unique. No matter how different we are, we're all going to die one day. They say your life flashes before your eyes when you're about to die, and when that day comes, and you're halfway down the digestive system of a bear or mountain lion, do you want to remember having lived your life based on what you wanted to do and by doing what you thought was right, or do you want to remember a life based on what other people told you to do, or not to do? You'll be in unimaginable agony either way, but still, imagine that it matters. Wouldn't your last minutes be happier if you were to revisit your life, and you saw yourself living your OWN life, based on your heart's promptings, instead of having lived it prodded on by the promptings of others? Wouldn't that ease the pain that the animal's razor sharp teeth are causing by pretty much ripping you apart?

Think of yourself as being a great big blob of musical notes. Everyone has the same notes, and everyone has the power to arrange them. Individuality isn't about having a different set of notes from one person to the next, it's just your way of rearranging the notes that makes you special. As Andie says in the movie Step Up 2: The Streets, "It's not about what you've got, it's what you make of what you've got."

But it shouldn't be like this either…

Grace Yan Sun

From Writing 100 (nominated by Simone Sessolo)

It is my great pleasure to nominate Grace Sun for the Sweetland Prize for Outstanding Portfolio. Grace enrolled in Writing 100 because she did not feel confident about her literacy level. However, from the first weeks of the semester, I noticed that her writing abilities were excellent, and she tackled each writing assignment with passion and dedication. She has been one of the strongest writers in my class.

During our one-on-one meetings, Grace told me that she had always given more attention to the sciences, and this lowered her confidence in writing. However, as a theme topic for the semester she decided to explore the consequences of global warming, and she could extend her attention and interest to many writing assignments, from research summaries to major papers. She also engaged in new media research, rhetorically analyzing a music video. Her ability to apply rhetorical appeals to visual media is impressive, and it shows that Grace has evolved into a considerate and confident writer.

Grace's e-portfolio is a great example of her development as a writer and a rhetorical thinker. Her attention to design and clarity is remarkable, and with her essays Grace is able to catch the attention of her readers. She also shows a lot of self-reflection, especially in her page "Personally." I hope you enjoy reading her e-portfolio as much as I did.

Simone Sessolo

To find my source, I typed in "global warming songs" into a Google search bar. With previous research summaries, I found myself getting bored with reading everything the author said and picking out parts that were important to their argument. I thought back to elementary school and how there were many songs about the environment we used to sing about and decided to look for a song that could fit my issue of global warming. I found a site that listed a few top songs about climate change. I scrolled through all of the songs, and Michael Jackon's "Earth Song" struck me as the most impactful because of the video that accompanied his music. To make sure I wanted to pick "Earth Song" as my source, I listened to the other songs and looked up their authors to check their credibility.

I found Jackson's song to be the most credible and most suited towards my issue because of all the artists I found on the site, he is the most well-known and the accompanied video is related to my issue. Jackson had previously produced songs about society (i.e. "We are the World") and is a respected artist. This time, his song was more climate-oriented. Although the lyrics Jackson wrote are not hyperbolic or exaggerated, the video portrays a burning field with a crimson horizon and a huge storm that seems to ravage the earth while in fact is restoring everything back to its natural state. These shots in the video are exaggerated, however it is to provide insight to what the world looked like before all of imposed human products. Other shots are "natural," in that they aren't grossly exaggerated. These shots include tractors working on deforestation, dry fields with dead animals, and a smog filled sky with depressed looking citizens.

The lyrics Jackson uses to portray his stance about the climate change are, "What have we done to the world. Look what we've done." That lyric is especially powerful because the video starts out with a sunny day in a healthy looking jungle, which is suddenly disrupted by a tractor that plows through the trees. As the video progresses, the world's state seems to deteriorate with flash backs to the past where the world wasn't so corrupted by humans. Nearing the last three minutes of the music video, Jackson increases the intensity of his voice where he repeats, "what about us?" in between other lyrics that question the health of the planet that shelters us and how current events are going to affect our posterity. To end his lyrics, Jackson screams, "Do we give a damn?" a question that catches the listener's attention if they hadn't been paying attention to the earlier "what about..." ones. These repeated lyrics give a sense of emphasis and will slowly become desensitized. Adding a "do we give a damn?" is a bold statement that will catch the attention of the viewers and receive it as a question to be thought about.

Works Cited

Brandt, Nick, dir. *Earth Song*. Perf. Michael Jackson. 1995. MJJ Productions Inc. Web. 10/28/12.

Considerations

There is no one who can argue that the earth has not changed in the past few decades. The question that remains is: how much and in what aspect? In the particular case of global warming, scientists, organizations, and other individuals all have their own take on this issue: global warming does exist, it doesn't exist, it does exist but the cause is not this particular source... etc. With all these positions, the pop-star Michael Jackson let his position be known in 1995 by producing *Earth Song* and its accompanying video with Nick Brandt: climate change has caused the world to turn for the worse.

Michael Jackson was one of the most famous musical artists in the world, known as the King of Pop. He had previously written other songs regarding world problems, such as *We Are the World.* The songs that address international issues are credible in that the songs emerge after the issue has been revealed to the world. Following his death, the Guinness World Records remember him as the philanthropic pop-star. In his lifetime, it was estimated that he donated 500 million dollars to charities. As he was one of the most famous artists and cared about the welfare of others, his influence on issues is powerful and he used it so in *Earth Song.*

Earth Song's logical argument follows a chronological sequence of events. The video sets out in a scenic shot, no signs of industrial disturbance. As the video progresses, the world becomes more corrupted to the point of regret. When this point is reached, the video plays a rewind as a storm sucking all the corrupted things away, leaving the happier times shown in the beginning. This chronological order of events allows the audience to see a bleak future that is undesirable in comparison to the beginning. After a certain number of events, the corruption of the world becomes clear and feelings of regret and despair are portrayed to the viewers. The storm is used to represent the force of the actions society could take now to prevent further exploitation of the Earth's resources.

Earth Song captures the topic of climate change as its video portrays images and shots that stir emotion within the audience. The video starts off as a beautiful, sunny day in the jungle. A panoramic shot captures multiple animals in their habitats, enjoying the sunlight and green canopy. The tranquility of the scene is abruptly disturbed by an unnatural smoky haze. This fog foreshadows the entrance of a rusty colored tractor that ploughs through the trees, doing its job of deforestation. The sudden appearance of the inorganic object produces feelings of intrusion. Something that so obviously does not belong in a scene will make anyone feel uncomfortable. The shot of the tractor moves closer to the audience until it runs the camera over. This is the very start of *Earth Song*'s video; no lyrics have been introduced and the only music heard is the sounds of nature and the roar of a machine.

After the tractor runs the camera over, giving an impression of running the audience over, the scene fades to black and transitions to a burning field of dead, cut-down trees. The view only consists of warm colors, but the association with these hues is something akin to hell. With just the colors, Brandt has created appealed to the senses in a way that would make the audience feel overwhelmed with heat and incensed, especially with the stark contrast with the previous scene of cool colors and a calming effect. The trees are blackened from the fire that still burns across sizzles the ground, and a dark pillar of smoke rises in the background. Michael Jackson makes his entrance here, starting his song with, "What about sunrise? What about rain? What about all the things/That you said we were to gain..." In the very few lines of his first stanza, Jackson criticizes a "you" figure, questioning the existence or state of simple things the world used to enjoy. The implications of the last completed phrase indicate a broken promise of gain, when in fact "we" experienced a great loss in a previous leisure provided by the environment.

The burning field gives way to a view of a dead elephant in a dried out field of sickly yellow. The view expands to include a dead baby elephant alongside the previous one and a nomad group surrounds the carcasses with expressions of sorrow. In this shot, the image of a familiar dead animal is a shocker. The rough, gray skin had peeled away from where the elephant's ivory tusks were taken to reveal the vulnerable red underneath. As if in anticipation of some apathy, Brandt expands the view to include the dead elephant's equally dead child next to it. This inclusion provides a relatable factor for all parents in the audience: the well-being of children. If the climate change has been so severe that it's affected families of other animals, what's not to say it won't affect human families?

After the scene with the elephants, the camera zooms in on one man as he looks off into the distance with dread. As the camera returns to Jackson, it only briefly stays on his face before the shot is panned upwards from the burning field into clouds of smoke, above which holds the beautiful blue sky and green canopy before it's switched back to Jackson staring past the camera where the audience sees the jungle again with the nomadic group. However, instead of the lush trees from the introduction, the trees shown here are in sparse numbers and in unhealthy condition as one of them falls near the nomadic group. The gaze of the man and Jackson rather than at the camera provides a feeling of the two thinking of times other than the present. For the man, staring off into the distance indicates a pensive thought for the future. While accompanied with the expression on his face, the anticipation of this future is filled with dread. Jackson's gaze upward implies thoughts to the past, before the invasive tendency of humans had corrupted the environment.

Progressive shots lead up to a grayscale scene of dejected looking citizens walking away from their reduced-to-rubble homes. A man sees a blackened, destroyed bicycle in the midst of stone and flashes back to a green field of laughing children and sunshine. He falls to his knees and the scene synchronizes with the nomadic group as they fall as well. The groups that fell are in despair, clutching at the dirt as Jackson vocalizes with aggravation. The sorrow tugs on the heartstrings of viewers as the video has shown the hardships they have endured. After the vocalization, Jackson starts with "I used to dream…" The scenes change to a blackened sky from industrialization, animals trapped and slaughtered which end in Jackson's continued vocalization that leads up to the storm that reverses time.. The quick-changing clips prompts shock and disbelief as the time for each shot is short, giving no time for the audience to process what they were just shown. In anticipating the storm, the song goes through a key change up to intensify the music. The storm rages on as Jackson's lyrics change to his accusations and questions of "What about us?" Through the storm, all that was corrupted is slowly brought back to its natural state. To tie the video in a circle, the elephant in the beginning is brought back to life with its ivory tusks intact as Jackson screams his last sentence "Do we give a damn?" The placement of these three lyrics are to impact the audience (etc)

Joseph Vogel, in Earth Song: Inside Michael Jackson's Magnum Opus, stated, "In place of nationalism, it [Earth Song] envisioned a world without division or hierarchy. In place of religious dogma or humanism, it yearned for a broader vision of ecological balance and harmony. In place of simplistic prop-aganda (sic) for a cause, it was a genuine artistic expression. In place of a jingly chorus that could be plastered on a T-shirt or billboard, it offered a wordless, universal cry" (Vogel, 5). This book was Vogel's perspective on Michael Jackson's development of *Earth Song* and Vogel's own analysis of the lyrics. With his quote above, Vogel asserts that *Earth Song* is not just another one of those advertisements that could be taken lightly. Jackson's artistic expression leaves an impact that cannot quite be duplicated. The song and video combination is so moving that nothing but its own entity can give the same message.

Global warming and climate change are big topics that most of society has at least heard about. Many individuals advocate their differing opinions, Michael Jackson, expressed his thoughts in music. Jackson's argument in *Earth Song* provided a visual impression of the world's corruption. Brandt utilizes a chronological argument to maximize logic and the swirl of emotions by the end of the video. By contrasting themes and different color palettes, Brandt is able to appeal to human emotions of anger, sympathy, empathy, discomfort, and many more that elicit a feeling to promote change. Together, Jackson and Brandt have created an impressionable artistic piece that speaks out against climate change.

Works Cited

Brandt, Nick, dir. *Earth Song*. Perf. Michael Jackson. 1995. MJJ Productions Inc. Web. 10/28/12.

Vogel, Joseph. *Earth Song: Inside Michael Jackson's Magnum Opus*. United States of America. BlakeVision Books. 2011. Print.

Earth Song. Dir. Nick Brandt. Perf. Michael Jackson. YouTube. YouTube, 22 Oct. 2009. Web. 11 Nov. 2012. <http://www.youtube.com/watch?v=XAi3VTSdTxU>.